Rapid Fire I

Hopping around some of Wester

Jason Smart

First English edition published in 2014 by Smart Travel Publishing

Cover design by Ace Graphics

ASIN: B00MR3HZYC
ISBN-13: 978-1500889364
ISBN-10: 1500889369

Smart, Jason J
Rapid Fire Europe: Hopping around some of Western Europe's favourite cities

For Aaron and Rachael

CONTENTS

Prologue

As my wife and I trudged through the hotel entrance in downtown Madrid, we were confronted by Jesus and the Germans. The trio of elderly Germans had gathered around Jesus to hear what he had to say. We listened too.

"Your room is on the third floor," harked Jesus. We knew he was Jesus due to the name tag on his blue uniform. "And the elevator is over there."

The Germans considered this, mentally scratching their heads. One of them, a bald individual with a pair of leathery lips spoke. "Thank you for explaining zis to us, but vee have many more questions." He turned to look at his companions. "This iz true, yah?"

They nodded and looked at Jesus.

Jesus looked pained but managed a thin smile. He evidently had the patience of a saint. The questions were all mundane but they came thick and fast. "Vill there be toast with the breakfast buffet? Vill vee be able to check out of our rooms late? And how many plug sockets vill the room have? And one last thing: vill vee be able to wear lederhosen for evening dinner tonight?"

The man called Jesus answered every question good-naturedly, even managing to smile as he did so. Eventually the Germans were satisfied, and shuffled towards the lift. It was now our time to bask in the presence of Jesus. He was a good man, and, in no time at all, had checked us into yet another room, in yet another country of Western Europe.

Introduction

The biggest problem with visiting Western Europe is the financial cost. Not the cost of getting there (though, of course, this can add up), but the simple cost of *being* there. There is no getting away from the fact that Western Europe is *expensive*, especially when visiting its cities, and the amount of euros, kroner and pounds needed for food and accommodation will mount up at such an alarming rate that daily visits to ATMs will become the norm. Buying a simple sandwich in Norway or a beer in Switzerland will bring a tear to the eye of all except the wealthiest of travellers. And the more countries visited, the worse this haemorrhaging of cash becomes.

Apart from the cash bleed, if anyone is foolhardy enough to want to visit country after country in Western Europe as I did, then there is the problem of logistics. Some smaller nations can be covered by a simple bus or train journey, and a few more can, if a person should want to undertake such folly, be hiked across in little more than a day; however for the most part, the quickest and often cheapest mode of transport is to fly. For the majority of my travels, I chose this method. Even so, planning my trip across multiple countries turned into a headache of epic proportions.

Onward connections, airport transfers and the occasional side trip proved so time-consuming that I decided to split my adventure into three manageable chunks: chunk one would see me visit thirteen different countries, covering most of Scandinavia and many of the smaller countries of Western Europe; chunk two would take in the Iberian Peninsula, as well as the UK, France and Ireland; the final segment would cover four additional European countries, all of them shivering in the grip of winter – an adventure taking me to twenty-two countries in all, with only Greece, Cyprus and Andorra managing to evade my ever-moving footsteps. And each of these trips would be a quick, rapid-fire visit. There would be no lingering in one place with so many nations to visit; I would be in each country for a maximum of two nights only: a snapshot of each.

The term *Western Europe* is sometimes a contentious issue. It dates from the Cold War, when countries not aligned to the Soviet Union were simply classed as the *West*. Times have changed: many former Soviet republics are now part of the EU and NATO, and some consider themselves part of Western Europe, or, at the very least, Central Europe. The term *Eastern Europe* is not well liked, primarily because of the images it conjures, usually of dour-faced men and women queuing up to buy simple provisions in grainy grey streets, and besides, as a blanket description for certain countries, it is geographically erroneous. Finland, for instance, a country generally considered part of Western Europe, lies further east than Hungary and Latvia. Greece is further east than the Czech Republic and most of Poland. Therefore, I use the term *Western Europe* in this book for the sake of simplicity. For me, it was a useful way to band countries together and saved me having to name this book *Rapid Fire Europe: Visiting the Cities of 22 Western, Southern, some Central, and a lot of Northern European Countries.*

And now the journey itself. In the north-west portion of a European map, tucked in between the tip of Scotland and the eastern edge of Greenland is a small but fun-filled island. This volcanic piece of rock holds the record for having the most northerly capital in Europe. It's also famous for its puffins and hotdogs. And, though the name of the country makes it sound cold and frigid, in actual fact, it is usually pleasantly warm and sunny in July. Its name is Iceland.

Part 1

Iceland, Norway, Switzerland, Liechtenstein, Malta, Monaco, Belgium, Luxembourg, The Netherlands, Denmark, Sweden, Italy, the Vatican

Chapter 1. Reykjavik, Iceland

Interesting fact: Many Icelanders believe in elves. Roads sometimes need to be rerouted to avoid disturbing them.

Iceland was somewhere I'd wanted to visit for a long time, but the cost had always put me off. A pint of beer for twelve pounds, a puffin fillet for thirty quid – Iceland was one of the most expensive places to visit in the world. Then something happened to change this outlook: the Icelandic krona took a nose dive and, overnight, Iceland became an affordable destination.

The Icelandair Boeing 757 delivered me punctually into Keflavik airport and I was soon aboard the Flybus heading into the city centre. The driver was a buxom blonde with rosy red cheeks. If she had been wearing animal hides, she could've passed as a Viking wife.

The countryside was rocky, hostile and mossy. Later I learned the rocks were lava deposits, a legacy from the island's volcanic heritage. The more I looked, the more rocks and lichen I could see, and then I realised the scenery reminded me of Scotland: dramatic and jagged, beautiful yet treacherous. Something caught my eye: a plume of smoke escaping from one of the distant peaks. The last thing I needed was to be stranded in Iceland while a cloud of ash blew over Europe grounding every flight in its wake. I muttered to myself in consternation.

"Are you looking at that ash flow?" asked a man's voice from the seat behind. His English diction was perfect, though with a slight accent. I turned to see a middle-aged gent in a business suit. Like the driver, he had rosy cheeks and a wide face: an Icelander.

I nodded and smiled.

"All tourists stare at the ash clouds. Do not worry. It will not cause any disruption for you. It is a normal occurrence in my country. By the way, my name is Magnus."

"I'm Jason." I said. "So eruptions like this are common?"

Magnus nodded. "But what you are looking at is not an eruption; it is just some gas escaping: a new born baby compared to the monster that grounded every flight a while ago. You remember that?"

I nodded again. For six days in April 2010, tens of thousands of flights across northern Europe had been cancelled. Twenty countries had shut down their airspace, creating an aircraft blackout not seen since the Second World War. It cost the airlines $1.7 billion in lost revenue and affected ten million people's travel plans. But it seemed a repeat of that event was not likely.

I began to read a tourist newspaper that had been left on the seat by a previous passenger. The mayor of Reykjavik, Jon Gnarr, wrote the article and the main thrust of his piece was to ask tourists to spend their money in Iceland. 'Spend, spend, spend' was his simple message: the only way the Icelandic economy could recover, he claimed

Another money-spinner for Iceland was its prime location. It was halfway across the Atlantic, mid-distance between Europe and North America. Icelandair had made great moves in establishing Reykjavik as a popular transit point between both continents, and indeed my flight from Manchester had been full, mostly with Americans. The elderly couple seated next to me were from the US city of Minneapolis. I knew this not because I'd spoken to them, but because I'd secretly read the ticket stub of the wife. I had no desire to speak to either of them because of what happened when I'd boarded the plane.

2

I was one of the last passengers to board the aircraft, and as I reached my row, I noticed the golden oldies immediately. The husband was sitting in the aisle seat eying me balefully as I manoeuvred my hand luggage into the overhead bin. His wife was sitting snugly in my seat (the window seat) leaving the middle one empty. They had obviously been hoping that the seat would remain empty. My presence had dashed that hope for them and now they hated me.

I looked at the woman and smiled. "Hi. You're in my seat, but if you want to stay by the window," I said, "that's fine." I directed my gaze to the husband. "So if you just move to the middle, I'll sit in the aisle."

The old goat's reaction surprised me. After grimacing, he wobbled a pair of large red lips over his gnashing teeth. "No, son!" he snarled. "I'm not moving one inch. I've got a bad leg!" He sat back and folded his arms, seemingly satisfied that he'd sorted me out. His wife glared too, and then looked out of the window.

Okay, I thought, two can play at this game. With a full aircraft, and a lot of people staring, I looked at the old man and gestured to the window seat. "Your wife is sitting in my seat. Out of courtesy to her, I don't mind if she stays there, but you need to move over."

"I said I'm not moving," he repeated in his Minneapolis drawl. "So don't ask again."

I was flabbergasted. The cheek of the old git! With forty pairs of eyes upon me, including both obstinate pensioners, I decided to play hardball. "Yes, you are. Both of you move so I can have my window seat."

The old couple looked at me with pure, undisguised loathing. I stood my ground until a member of the cabin crew came over, checked my ticket stub, and asked them to move too. It took a while, but I waited patiently. As I settled down in my warm window seat, I mentally crossed Minneapolis off from places to visit in the US. Neither of the pensioners looked at me for the rest of the flight, which was fine by me.

3

Reykjavik was sunny and pleasantly warm by the time I arrived at my hotel. I didn't have to worry about the sun going down because sunset was around midnight in the summer months. After unpacking a few things, I left the hotel and found myself in a small square called Ingolfstorg. It was full of skateboarding teenagers and steam vents. I wandered towards the sea, enjoying the warm, fresh air of Iceland.

The Sun Voyager is one of the most photographed sculptures in the city. Made of steel, the skeletal Viking ship sculpture was in a prominent position overlooking the harbour. It looked incredible, resembling a fish skeleton made from silver, except boat-shaped. It was surprisingly large and, while I marvelled at the way sunlight caught the steel ribs, a young couple arrived and stood waiting for me to finish taking a photo. I did, and then stood staring out across the bay. The opposite side of the inlet looked brooding and uninviting; long, flat-topped hills shrouded in grey mist: the abode of monsters – monsters that ate woolly mammoths and chewed on Viking skulls. Feeling a slight chill in the air, I turned heel and headed inland.

4

The Hallgrimskirkja Church jutted into the sky for 75 metres, making it the third-tallest building in Iceland. It looked like no other church I'd seen, full of sweeping, graceful angles that led up to the majestic white tower. It was one of the most striking churches I had ever laid my eyes upon and I simply could not stop staring. Other people were gazing upwards too, and, to take advantage of the crowds, a mobile hotdog vendor had set up shop on the road opposite. He was doing brisk business.

I ignored the hotdogs and wandered to a large statue in front of the church. It was of Leif Ericson, an Icelandic Viking who had discovered the New World five hundred years before Columbus. Standing with his chin turned to the elements and a large battle axe by his side, Ericson looked the epitome of a Norse hero.

For 600 krona (£3), I bought a ticket to the observation deck inside Hallgrimskirkja's mighty tower. The views were stunning, covering the entire city and beyond. Reykjavik was a low-rise city, and many of the buildings had red, green and white roofs, giving them an almost toy-town feel. And the air was beautifully clean; I could see for miles, into the far reaches of the gun-grey Atlantic Ocean. Suddenly an almighty racket above our heads broke the peace. The church bells were chiming for 7pm. For me, it signalled time for food, followed by rest in the hotel. I had a full day the next day, the first of many in the coming weeks.

5

The next morning was grey and drizzly, the exact opposite of the previous evening. Around the corner from the hotel was another little square. In the centre was a statue of a stately looking gentleman standing on a tall plinth. The same man's portrait also graced the front of the 500-krona note. His name was Jón Sigurðsson, a politician who had championed Icelandic independence in the nineteenth century. Appropriately enough, he was standing opposite the parliament building.

The building where important Icelandic legislature was discussed was a splendid two-storey grey structure completely devoid of security guards. Had I wanted to, I could have skipped to the wooden doors and knocked on them, or even tapped on the windows. Wondering whether to do exactly that, I heard voices behind me. A small tour group of pensioners had arrived and were now congregating around the Sigurðsson statue. All of them were listening to their female guide.

The woman stopped speaking as I approached, and everyone looked at me. I nodded and smiled, but when I received nothing back, I pretended to take a photo. What was it with pensioners in Iceland, I wondered? All of them seemed miserable to the extreme. As I framed my shot of the statue, the group waited, with no one speaking, and so, afterwards, I decided to loiter a little longer, just to annoy them. First I tied my shoelace and then I stood up and regarded the sky. Was it going to rain, I pondered? I held out my hand to test for droplets and, once satisfied that it was not, I fished the guidebook from my pocket. After flicking backwards and forwards a couple of time, the guide finally gave up and resumed her monologue, but this time at an almost whisper. I decided it was too much effort to listen and instead walked over to the small church next door to the parliament building.

It was actually Reykjavik's oldest church, but I did not feel like lingering due to the God-awful stench. The large drainage truck parked in front seemed the culprit. With a lovely aroma of fresh sewage being sucked up from the city's bowels, I decided to head towards the harbour. It was time to search out some puffins.

6

The harbour area was the oldest part of the city and it was here that fishing boats and yachts vied for position along the jetties. I also passed four large black ships that looked ominous in the grey water. And ominous they indeed were, for they were Icelandic whaling ships. Whaling is still big business in Iceland, despite most of Western Europe being aghast at the idea. Between these four ships, dozens of whales are killed each year. I left the black whalers behind and came to a booth offering puffin boat tours.

"I'm sorry, sir," said the young woman on the other side of the hatch. Like all people in Iceland, her English was flawless. "The puffin boat has just left. You have missed it by ten minutes. But you probably would not have seen the puffins anyway. The previous trip came back without seeing any, which is unusual. However, if you like, I could book you on this afternoon's tour?"

"Do you think the puffins will be around then?"

The woman shrugged. "I can't say...but probably not. How about this? You come back in one hour and I'll let you know whether the current tour group saw any puffins. If they do, I will book you on the next trip for half price. If they don't, then you can go on your way. How does that sound?"

I smiled. What an unbelievably kind offer. I thanked her and said I would return in an hour. So, to pass the time, I wandered back into the town centre, browsing the shops and cafes along the main street, keeping a wary look out for elderly Americans.

Reykjavik definitely had a small-town vibe, and seemed content to bask in its heritage. The buildings all looked old but exquisitely well kept. Some featured wooden shutters and most were painted in gorgeous pastel colours. Also, quite remarkably for a capital city in Europe, Reykjavik didn't have any Starbucks or MacDonald's. The burger-making giant had pulled out of Iceland in 2009 following the financial crash. It has no plans to return either, claiming that the 'unique operational complexity' of operating its business model in an isolated island country, with a population of just 320,000, was simply too difficult to manage. A local burger chain, *Metro*, took up the slack. It made me realise I was hungry, but, instead of a burger, I decided to go for a hotdog. But not just any hotdog: a hotdog fit for an American president.

7

After some hasty map reading, I found myself joining the lengthy queue at Baejarins Beztu Hotdog stand. Unlike most other hotdog stands (and there were plenty of them in Reykjavik), Baejarins Beztu's was a bona fide tourist attraction, with people actually taking photos of themselves in the queue. The reason for this was simple: Bill Clinton had once visited Iceland and enjoyed one of Reykjavik's finest from this very van. To prove it, a photo of him eating it had been placed on a nearby wall. In 2006, *The Guardian* newspaper declared that Baejarins Beztu's hotdogs were the best in Europe. I joined the back of the queue in anticipation.

"350 krona," said the woman inside the red and white van, the same woman who had served Mr Clinton, as far as I could tell. She'd also served the lead singer from Metallica, at least judging from the nearby photo. I paid the lady and I took my hotdog to a nearby wall, where I sat down and took a bite, tasting the familiar taste of hotdog and ketchup. It was quite nice and I quickly took a second bite, and then a third. Soon it was gone.

There was a middle-aged couple sitting a bit further along from me. The man turned to me. "Good hotdog, yah?"

His accent sounded German, or perhaps Dutch. I nodded. "Yeah, tasty."

The man considered this and so did his wife. She looked like she ought to be called Helga, all buxom and stout. He said, "I wonder, though, did you taste anything special in your hotdog? Something perhaps...*different?*"

"Different? No. It just tasted like a regular hotdog."

"Yah. Regular hotdog. That is what I think too. I am saying this to my wife that I cannot understand why these hotdogs are so famous. We have better ones in Cologne."

I nodded, not knowing what to say. Instead, I got up, said goodbye and set off walking back to the puffin lady.

8

"They didn't see a single puffin," she told me. "A bad day for puffin spotting."

I shook my head and looked out to sea. There were lots of birds out there; all of them squawking as they flew around the boats or sat perched on their masts. However, all of them were normal seagulls and not the prize I'd been hoping for.

"Perhaps you can try again tomorrow?" the woman suggested.

"I can't. I'm flying to Oslo."

"Oh, well, if you are ever back in Reykjavik, then please try again. Our tours normally see puffins. Like I said earlier, it is very unusual..."

I thanked the woman and wandered away. And then I had an idea; if I couldn't see a puffin in its natural habitat, I would order a cooked one on a plate later that evening. That would serve them right.

To work up an appetite, I decided to take a two-kilometre hike to a strange place called Perlan. Halfway there, the heavens rudely opened: a deluge that had been brewing all morning. My head was blasted with a fountain of cold rain, and water started sloshing down my neck. Cursing my lack of umbrella, I pulled a woolly hat from my pocket and put it on my head. With my eyes fixed ahead, I trudged onwards.

Perlan was a large domed structure that housed a special museum. Despite loathing museums, I thought a visit to a Viking-themed one would be interesting; besides, I now needed somewhere to dry out. After dripping water onto the floor of the large open-plan entrance hall, which garnered a few glances, I paid the entrance fee to the Saga Museum. The teenager who sold me a ticket asked if I wanted an audio guide, but I told him that I would be my own guide. The boy barely glanced at me. *Whatever*, his look said, as he pointed to the entrance before returning to his mobile phone.

Inside, the Saga Museum was dark and I got a shock when I turned the first corner and came face to face with a large Viking. Thankfully, he was made of wax and so I moved past him, allowing my eyes to adjust to the lack of light. The makers of the museum had made lots of other wax people, all kitted out in Viking attire: one in particular caught my eye, because it was a bare-breasted Viking woman. According to the information placard, the woman had been battling invaders and, in desperation, had exposed her chest to her assailants. This daring tactic worked because her attackers had apparently fled.

Everyone apart from me was wearing headphones. The nine or ten people inside the museum were intently listening to their audio guide, pausing at choice moments to hear the appropriate narrative. I sidestepped one family and stopped to look at a waxwork woman about to be burned at the stake, and then at another of an old man about to have his head chopped off. Suitable sound effects were being piped in from hidden speakers, and I tuned into the screams and burning noises. They sounded suitably authentic.

Further along was a Viking family inside their hovel, but one of the figures was not made of wax: he was a real man. His movements were almost imperceptible, but I spotted them nonetheless. He was one of those actors who waited until he had a sizeable audience before jumping out to cause panic and hilarity. I pretended I hadn't noticed him and moved to the adjacent exhibit where I waited for him to work his magic. The family I'd passed earlier came along and stood looking at the display. I waited for the actor to terrify them, but he was not obliging. After a minute more, I gave up and left, exiting the museum precisely nine minutes after entering. That was when I heard the scream.

9

That evening, I paid a visit to the appropriately named Icelandic Bar. The menu offered puffin for 4500 krona (£23). When the young waitress came over, I asked her what it tasted like.

"It's a dark meat," she told me, "a bit like beef, and nothing like chicken as you might have expected. But it is tasty. However, if you're thinking of ordering it, I'm afraid we don't have any."

What was it with Icelandic puffins? There were none in the wild and none in its fridges. I perused the menu, wondering what else I could have, and my eyes soon found an item of food I'd never sampled before: whale meat. After some mental to-ing and fro-ing, I ordered some. Twenty minutes later, it arrived, and as I looked at the smoked strips of minke whale, I couldn't rid myself of the image of a beautiful, graceful and highly intelligent mammal swimming about in the ocean, perhaps with a calf by its side. It was horrible to imagine that such an elegant creature had been butchered so a few slices of meat could appear on my plate. I had absolutely no appetite for whale meat now, and so, to summon up some courage, I took a sip of my Viking beer. Afterwards, I hesitantly picked up my fork and pressed it into one of the deep-red slithers of flesh.

As I chewed on the piece of whale meat, I decided the texture was like salmon, albeit a bit tougher, and the taste was remarkably similar too. I tried to imagine it *was* salmon, but the damage had been done; I couldn't eat any more. I put down my fork and pushed my plate away.

The waitress reappeared a few minutes later and saw the almost-full plate. "Not good for you?" she asked. She didn't seem surprised.

I decided to tell the truth. "There's nothing wrong with it. And I'm glad I've tried it...but I just can't..."

The girl nodded and smiled. "Many visitors to Reykjavik say the same thing: they want to try whale but then cannot actually eat it."

"So whale is popular with tourists?" I had assumed it was on the menu for the locals.

"We sell almost half our whale meat to tourists."

On the way back to my hotel, I thought about what the waitress had told me. If people such as me were ordering whale meat in Iceland, then we were fuelling the country's whaling industry, sending the black ships out to capture and kill. It was a horrible thought.

I arrived back at my hotel with daylight still streaming through the windows. The next day, my short time in Iceland would come to an end and I'd not even had time to visit the world-famous Blue Lagoon, the geothermal spa southwest of the capital. Despite this, I'd really enjoyed my visit to Reykjavik; it reminded me of an upmarket British seaside town, without the tattooed and lobster-coloured arms. As for the puffins, they had won the battle this time. But perhaps that was a good thing. My whale experience had put me off exotic meats for the time being. I closed the thick curtains and sat down with my guidebook to Western Europe. It was time to read about my next destination: Oslo.

Top row: The Sun Voyager; Baejarins Beztu Hotdog stand
Middle row: Bear-breasted Viking woman in the Saga Museum;
The pretty houses of downtown Reykjavik;
Bottom row: Hallgrimskirkja Church; An Icelandic warrior

Chapter 2: Oslo, Norway

Interesting fact: Boxing was banned on Norwegian TV until the late eighties.

It was my own fault, of course. When I first arrived at Oslo Central Station from the airport, I'd done the sensible thing and walked straight for a waiting taxi. While listening to my request to take me to the Radisson hotel, the driver held up a hand to stop me talking. "If I were you," he said in English so perfect that I couldn't detect any accent, "I would walk. Your hotel is not far. It's just up and around that street." He pointed to where he meant. "But if you do want a ride, then please get in. The price is 150 kroner."

Fifteen pounds for a journey that sounded like a five-minute walk seemed insane. I thanked the helpful cab driver and set off along the horrendously busy street, a small rucksack strapped across my shoulder, a coat hung under my arm, and a heavy suitcase trailing behind like a dead weight.

It was busy because it was six pm and Osloites were heading home after a day's work. I rounded the bend the taxi driver had pointed at and, after negotiating an endless stream of pedestrians and trams, I stopped to get my bearings. There was no sign of the Radisson. I checked around another corner, but there was nothing. With the sun beating down, dazzling my weary eyes, I started cursing the cab driver.

As I turned another bend, the crowds thinned and so did my sense of direction. I was wandering aimlessly. Fifteen minutes later, I admitted defeat and entered a dimly-lit bar to ask for directions. The man behind the counter listened to my tale of woe and soon had me on my way. Almost one hour after leaving the train station, I arrived at the Radisson Blue hotel, hot and bothered, but with 150 kroner still in my wallet.

2

After a quick shower, I felt ready to brave the streets of Oslo again. I studied my map and worked out my route back to the centre of town. The taxi driver had been correct, the hotel was just around the corner from the train station, and how I'd ended up so lost was a mystery.

After the almost provincial feel of Reykjavik, Oslo was back to the bustling major city. The focal point was most definitely Stortinget, the fabulous parliament building. It was bathed in amber as the evening sunlight caught its rounded facades. Hordes of people were hanging around the front of it, or ambling by with helium-filled balloons and ice-creams.

Oslo was no slouch when it came to statues; they were all over the joint. Moreover, the city was also teeming with fountains and bars. The latter were crowded with people drinking and eating, and I decided to sit in an outdoor bar overlooking Stortinget. As I sat enjoying a pint of Ringnis lager with a cheeseburger, I found myself in an agreeable mood. Rapid Fire Europe was in its second country, and all had gone well. And then the bill arrived.

Thirty bloody quid! The beer alone was over ten pounds! And twenty quid for a simple cheeseburger? What the hell was going on? I knew Norway was going to be expensive, but this was another league, perhaps the most expensive country I'd ever visited. It was a good job I'd saved my taxi fare. Later, I discovered that the most expensive Big Macs in the world are Norwegian ones. According to data collected in January 2012, a Big Mac in Oslo would set a person back 59 kroner, which was almost ten dollars. Compare this to the cheapest Big Mac in Europe, over in Ukraine. There, a McDonald's finest would cost someone only $2.11. But then again, the average monthly salary in Norway is about ten times that of Ukraine.

To take my mind off the way my money was disappearing, I walked away from Stortinget until I saw some Hare Krishnas. Five of them were sitting on the ground, singing away and shaking various percussion instruments, all with impressive gusto. A small crowd had gathered around them, but I moved on, making my way towards a building that had made world news in 2011.

3

On Friday 22 July 2011, at a quarter past three in the afternoon, a young policeman had parked a white Volkswagen van near the front entrance of a tall governmental building. The structure housed the Norwegian president's offices, as well as some offices of the Ministry of Justice.

After switching off the engine, the bogus officer climbed out of the van and stood by it for a few seconds, as if pondering his next move. Finally, he walked briskly away to another street where an empty parked car waited for him. When the man arrived at the second car, he jumped in and drove westwards.

Back near the president's office, a secretary working in the government building noticed the white van and became worried about its presence. As she made a phone call, a bomb contained within the van exploded, ripping through every building along the street, blowing out window after window, killing the secretary and seven other people. Hundreds more were injured, but the death toll could have been much worse: because it was a Friday afternoon, it meant an early finish for many government workers, and many of them had already left.

Heading west, meanwhile, the man masquerading as a police officer was still up to no good. One and half hours after leaving behind the carnage in the city centre, he arrived on the island of Utoya. Once there, Anders Breivik shot and killed a further 69 people, most of them teenagers. Once the police arrested him, Norway went into immediate mourning. Breivik was sentenced to 21 years in prison.

I stared at the street where Anders Breivik had parked his white van, unable to imagine the horror he had unleashed. I recalled watching the news in the hours and days following the attacks.

Oslo had become a city of flowers. Roses of every colour were placed on every street, on every fence, and on virtually every statue. Behind Oslo Cathedral lay a huge field of roses, stretching out until the individual blooms became a single sea of colour.

I returned to my hotel in a sombre mood.

4

The next morning was warm and sunny. After stopping off at an ATM to get more kroner, I took a detour towards the Royal Palace, home of the current monarch, King Harald V.

A Japanese tour group had beaten me to it, all of them posing and taking photos in front of the palace. One young man, who should have known better, was standing on one leg with his tongue out. His girlfriend was giggling as she took a photo of him. Another man was taking a photo of his wife, who was on the steps. Normal enough, except for one thing: the woman was holding a green plastic frog in the air.

I was surprised about the lack of barriers and guards around the palace. Unlike, say, Buckingham Palace, it looked possible to walk up to the royal building itself. In fact, it seemed like a few people were doing exactly that. I watched them as they made their way to a small booth containing a guard who was wearing a silly feather hat. Then they took a few photos. Apart from the guard, there seemed a distinct lack of security, which was a refreshing outlook, I thought, especially in a city that had gone through hell.

Turning around, I regarded the tall red brick towers of Oslo City Hall, the place where Nobel Peace Prizes were given out. Fifteen minutes later, I was walking underneath their shadows as I entered its great hall. Inside City Hall was a gallery of sorts. Lots of large-scale paintings, including a scene of frolicking naked people, were all around. In another room, a gigantic picture showed people being attacked by huge insects. A young Korean woman entered and screamed, covering her face in a picture of absolute shock. She left soon after. It wasn't surprising; one bleak section showed a man being assaulted by a giant earwig. For quite a few moments I was unable to tear my eyes away from the dreadful scene. Finally, I turned around and headed back outside.

5

Aker Brygge is the bustling, renovated harbour district of Oslo. It had once been an old shipyard, but nowadays is the home to large-masted boats, small ferries and numerous pleasure craft. After grabbing a take away coffee, I joined a small line of people to board one boat that would take me to the Bygdoy Peninsula, home of the famous Viking Ship Museum.

The ten-minute journey was uneventful and I was one of the first passengers to disembark. After getting my bearings, I headed up a steep, tree-lined street; some of my fellow passengers spotted my decisive move and started following me. I felt like waving them off, or at least warning them not to trail me due to my notoriously poor sense of direction, but, instead of doing that, I became the Pied Piper of Oslo and carried on up the hill.

At the top, I came to a fork in the road. I stopped to read my map and noticed my acolytes had also slowed, waiting for me to lead them onwards. I looked this way and that, trying to spot any identifiable features; after failing to do so, I elected for the left fork. My followers followed. Five minutes later, I spied a large building, which looked like it might be a museum. A couple of picnic tables and parasols, together with a group of people hanging around, led me to believe it was the Viking Ship Museum. It was, and I walked towards the entrance with my followers close behind.

For less than the price of an Oslo beer, I was in the museum, marvelling at the Oseberg and Gokstaf Viking ships, as well as a third one, Tune, which, to be honest, looked like a pile of broken wood. The first two were the finest preserved examples of Viking ships anywhere in the world – long and sleek, looking every inch

Viking. They towered above me and it was hard to imagine that they were both over a thousand years old.

The museum was full of tourists, and I looked for the people who had followed me up the hill. I saw some of them around the other side of a long Viking oar; I wondered whether they were waiting for me to leave, so they could trail after me again. If so, they would have to hurry up, because I was going right now. After one quick circuit of the Oseberg, I was off, pausing only to grab a can of cola from the stall outside. I tried not to wince when I handed over a 50 kroner note (£5) and received no change in return.

6

My phone rang. It was my wife, Angela. She wanted to know where I was and how I was getting on. I told her I was still in Norway and I'd spent about one hundred and fifty pounds since arriving.

"A hundred and fifty pounds? You've been there less than a day! What have you spent it all on?"

"Nothing really. A museum, a few meals, a couple of beers, oh, and last night, on the way back to the hotel, I bought a Snickers bar. That cost £3.50! You need to be a millionaire to live here."

"My God! So what's Oslo like? Is it full of blonde-haired people?"

I looked around. I was back in downtown Oslo: Aker Brygge, to be precise. "Yeah, there are quite a lot of blonde people. But I'll tell you something: a lot of the women here have their boobs out. I can see one woman right now. She's standing in front of me. She's topless."

Angela didn't say anything.

"Did you hear what I said?"

"Yes."

"And there's woman with her chest out a bit further along too. She's sprawled out with two kids playing by her feet. It's shameless...I don't know where to look."

I could hear Angela sighing. "So you're staring at statues?"

I chuckled. "They're everywhere. Most are indecent."

After saying goodbye, and then scoffing a wallet-destroying sandwich, I climbed up to the grounds of Akershus Fortress, Oslo's medieval castle. Like all good castles, it had round towers, lofty battlements and some tall spires poking upwards from its centre. I had a good look around and, as I walked through a medieval archway into a small courtyard, I heard a man's raised voice. He was standing in the middle of the courtyard with a small boy (his son, presumably). The boy was staring at the floor at an upturned ice-cream on the ground.

"I told you to watch where you were going!" said the man, in an American accent. "Now look what's happened."

The ice-cream had landed almost vertically, making it resemble one of the medieval turrets above my head. It looked quite comical, though neither father nor son looked in any way amused. I turned away from the drama and headed back down the steps to Aker Brygge. It was late afternoon, I was thirsty and I needed a drink.

7

I found a bar with a shady table. As I took a sip of my 90 kroner beer, I noticed a savvy young couple sat on a nearby bench. The woman produced a few slices of bread from her bag and a foil packet of something; she then proceeded to make a ham sandwich. The couple sat eating, content in the knowledge that they had saved themselves about fifty quid.

Later that evening, I decided to visit Oslo's National Gallery. It was either that or catching a bus to Vigeland Park, described in the guide book as being a must-see sight. But with time ticking away, I elected for the art.

For the eleven minutes I spent inside the art gallery, I focussed my attention on two aspects of art. One was a nude statue of a woman I rather liked, and the other was Edvard Munch's best-known piece, *The Scream*. Judging by the look on the main character's face, he had just received his bill in an Oslo restaurant.

Munch is Norway's most famous painter, but it wasn't until he was thirty that Munch painted his most recognisable piece. I was surprised to learn that there were in fact four versions of The Scream, produced some 17 years apart. The one I was staring at was the first one, dating from 1893.

Right, I thought, that's it. Time to go. My day in the Norwegian capital had come to an end. And perhaps that was a good thing; I'd spent a ridiculous sum of money. I was certainly hoping that my next port of call was going to be easier on the wallet, though I seriously doubted it. Zurich was supposed to be another notoriously expensive city in Western Europe. I headed back to the Radisson to pack.

Top row: Parliament building; Me enjoying a pint of expensive Norwegian lager
Middle row: Oslo is teeming with nude statues; The Royal Palace
Bottom row: Looking towards Akershus Fortress; Oslo City Hall – home of scary pictures

Chapter 3. Zurich, Switzerland

Interesting fact: According to the Economist Intelligence Unit, Switzerland is the best place to be born, due to its happiness, low crime rate and fine chocolate shops.

To be quite honest, I didn't know what to expect of Zurich, the largest city in Switzerland. In the past, Zurich had always been a stopover on the way to somewhere else. I'd have a coffee in the airport or maybe a sandwich, and then I'd be on my way, vaguely thinking of cuckoo clocks and Alpine skiing. But not this time. I had arrived in Zurich to see Zurich, so, instead of heading to airport transfers, I made my way towards passport control and then the exit. Ten minutes later, I was sitting on the airport train into the centre of the city, and by the time I arrived into Zurich's central train station, evening had turned into night. Feeling worn out by so much travel, I simply walked to the hotel, and, after a bite to eat in a Chinese restaurant across the road, I retired to my room with my guidebook and bottle of Swiss beer.

2

My visit to Zurich, like all other cities on my tour, was going to be a swift one. With only one full day in Switzerland, I was pleased when the morning was sunny and warm. After a lengthy walk downhill – passing, among other things, a hairdresser, an air-conditioning-unit shop and a large building called the Habib Bank Zurich – I arrived in the old town of Zurich. It was gorgeous: as simple as that.

It reminded me of Prague, or perhaps Tallinn, and, from my vantage point near the train station, I gawped at the charming bridges spanning the River Limmat, and at the beautiful church spires that rose up above the medieval guild houses. Cobblestone paths led upwards and then disappeared into picturesque alleyways, and trams crisscrossed the busy main streets below. Zurich was a real beauty, and I wondered why I'd never thought about visiting it before. It was hard to believe that, in the 1980s, Zurich had been one of the drug capitals of Europe. One of its parks had even been dubbed Needle Park because of the addicts who congregated there.

A seedy element to the city still existed, though. In one pamphlet I'd looked at in the hotel, the rear section was full of advertisements for adult clubs and escort agencies. One establishment boasted that it was 'Switzerland's finest Escort Agency' and had 'more than forty ladies available to give pleasure to the gentleman'. Another described its 'beautiful, classy and elegant' ladies, and also mentioned that the women were 'cultivated'. Cultivated from what, it didn't say. I quickly noted down the address and was soon on my way.

3

Except, of course, I wasn't. I was in Zurich to see the gorgeous old town, as were plenty of others. Catering to the sightseeing hordes were parades of tour buses, some of them the open-topped variety. I ignored a tout waving at me and made my way to the Gates of Hell.

The Gates of Hell were where I'd probably have ended up had I paid a visit to that escort agency, but these particular Gates of Hell were amazing. The sculpture was on the outside wall of the Kunsthaus, one of Zurich's premier art galleries, and was twenty feet tall. It consisted of a large, black and intricately decorated piece of work by the renowned French artist Auguste Rodin. It took him almost forty years to finish: not surprising, since the scene contained an incredible 180 individual figures, all of them twisting and writhing in perpetual agony. One man looked like he was having his ears pulled off.

After a short hike, I arrived at the city's most prominent landmark, Grossmunster, the mammoth twin-towered church that had been built on the site of an ancient Roman burial ground. At the top of both towers were some large Swiss flags swaying heartily in the breeze. I was about to go in, but a church service was in operation, and so instead I headed towards the edge of Lake Zurich, the expanse of water teeming with yachts, pedalos, swans, ducks and tour boats. The jetties were full of people too, queuing in horrendous lines to board sightseeing boats. I contented myself with ambling along the water's edge, nodding at a violin player standing under the shade of a tree as I passed him. Bratwurst and hotdog stands were in attendance too; I looked at my watch and saw it was almost lunchtime; five minutes later, I was eating a hotdog, my second in one week. It was almost identical to the one I'd eaten in Reykjavik, except for the price. My Swiss hotdog was double the price of its Icelandic counterpart.

Near the Town Hall, I spotted a couple of giggling teenage girls. One was posing while the other tried to take the photo. When they finally finished and moved on, I spotted why. Written on a public toilet door was the word: *pissoir*. I took a photo myself and then made use of the facilities.

4

Zurich's main shopping street is Bahnhofstrasse, a place my wife would have adored. Large department stores and designer goods shops line the wide street: an endless parade of shoes, bags and clothes, but I walked past every one without pause. I was on my way to Lindenhof Hill, the site of the ancient Roman castle.

Zurich had once been an important Roman settlement known as Turicum. The Romans built a fortress on top of a hill and used it to collect taxes. Nowadays, the almost circular hilltop area is devoted to greenery and benches with a waterfall thrown in for good measure. The castle is long gone, but the views are still impressive:

the same vista Roman soldiers would have seen from the fortress walls. The only evidence I could find that I was standing on a former Roman ruin was a stone replica of a Roman tombstone.

I decided it was time for a beer and chose a cafe overlooking the river. A white-shirted waiter appeared within a minute, ready to take my order. After I ordered, the man's response surprised me.

The waiter nodded and smiled. "Aye, man!" His accent was perfect Geordie. "I'll bring it over in just a minute, pal."

When he returned, we chatted. I found out his name was Jonathan and he was from Newcastle, not far from my home town of Middlesbrough. He asked me what I thought of Zurich.

I said, "Before coming here, I knew nothing about Zurich. Absolutely nothing. I didn't think there would be anything to see."

Jonathan nodded. "Aye, man. Same here. But it's a great city. I love it. And the only reason I came over was to stay with a friend of mine. But I ended up liking the place so much that I decided to stay. I got a job in this cafe."

"So you can speak German?" The majority of Zurich's inhabitants spoke German; English, I'd found out, was spoken surprisingly little in the city.

Jonathan nodded. "I studied it at school in Newcastle. But that was about ten years ago. But it's surprising what you can remember. Mind you, working in a cafe is great for language skills. I've soon picked it up again."

An elderly couple arrived and Jonathan invited me to enjoy my drink as he went off to serve them. I listened as he switched fluently to German while I sipped on Swiss lager from a vantage point that offered a great view of the spires and pointy roofs of an unexpectedly splendid European city.

5

My next sight was another church, this one called Fraumunster. Inside was an impressive set of organ pipes and some beautiful stained glass windows, so I decided to take a photo. As I angled for a shot of Christ on a sublime aquamarine background, I heard a tut. Ignoring it, I took a second photo and this time heard a sigh and then another tut. I lowered my camera and turned around to see a group of pensioners all staring at me. One man was shaking his head, gesturing to a sign. I looked at it. *No Photography*, it clearly stated. I must have missed it on the way in. I thanked the man, took a photo of the sign and disappeared through the door.

The weather was still gloriously sunny, the sort of day that everyone in England hoped for but seldom got. I sauntered along the riverbank, passing an open-air restaurant where a live jazz band was banging out an up-tempo number involving high-pitched trumpet flurries and dextrous double bass playing. I found a bench so I could listen to them. Jazz music wasn't my thing, but I could certainly appreciate the musicianship going into the number. Just then, the oldest couple in Zurich wandered past.

The stylish old gent was wearing a purple-checked jacket and matching tie. In one hand, he carried a long and sturdy walking cane. He looked about ninety years old. His equally elderly wife was by his side, walking with stooped back. Like her ancient husband, she was wearing her Sunday best, with the extra sartorial addition of a pair of white trainers.

Despite their advanced age, they moved in a sprightly fashion, until they stopped at a window display of a Swiss chocolatier. A teenager on a skateboard zoomed by them. That was the thing about Zurich: both young and old could enjoy it. I waited for the band to finish their piece and then stood up to find pastures new.

6

The Water Church's name came about because it had been originally constructed on a small island at the confluence of Lake Zurich and the River Limmat. Over time, someone had built a quay, which was great for me because, instead of having to catch a boat to it, I could simply walk to the medieval church.

I regarded the Water Church's exterior and decided it looked boring. It was a typical-looking old brown church, the same as thousands of others in Europe, and it was easily overshadowed by the gigantic towers of the Grossmunster behind it. But what made it interesting was its juicy history. According to legend, a couple of Roman soldiers named Felix and Regula (who were twin brothers) had been going about their business in the third century when they decided to convert to Christianity. This didn't go unnoticed by their superiors and they were promptly arrested and, because it was such a serious crime in those days, condemned to death.

On the day of their execution, guards led Felix and Regula from their cells to a crowded central square in the settlement that would eventually become Zurich. A couple of brutes with large axes were waiting for them. After the twins were given the opportunity to say a few final words, the executioners made the brothers kneel down on a stone tablet and then raised their sharpened axes.

At this point in the proceedings, it is not unreasonable to assume that someone in the crowd might have been praying for a miracle. After all, some spectators may well have been secret Christians, but, as the axe blades came down and made contact with the twins' necks, it seemed all was lost, especially when the two heads came cleanly off and rolled bloodily across the cobbles.

Then something odd happened.

Instead of collapsing in a dreadful pool of blood and sinew, the bodies of Felix and Regula shakily stood up. As people watched, mouths agape, the bloodied corpses walked over to their missing heads and picked them up. Then, rather like a pair of pantomime ghosts, they carried them under their arms and exited the square. As people blinked and slapped their foreheads in open astonishment, the corpses lumbered along for about forty metres before they faltered and stopped. With a crowd of horrified onlookers, the brothers knelt down, put their heads by their side, and then assumed a praying position. Only then did they finally fall down and die.

Because of these shenanigans, Felix and Regula become patron saints of the city. Grossmunster was built on the spot where they died, and the stone, where they were reputedly beheaded upon, formed the basis of the Water Church's crypt. I rushed up to the entrance in eager anticipation, but the door was locked. I tried it again but nothing was forthcoming. I looked at the sign next to the door and read that the crypt was closed because it was a Sunday. Damn and blast.

7

Later that evening, I was back in the old town, content at simply wandering the cobblestoned streets. With a low sun bathing the buildings in a delicious glow, Zurich looked at its most beautiful: a real contender for a wonderful European city break. I moved away from the riverfront, finding myself on a side street busy with outdoor restaurants and bars. Most were full, but one had a spare table, at which I sat down. When my beer arrived, I took a sip and felt supremely content. And then I thought about what I was doing the next day and felt even better. I was going to Liechtenstein, a place few people had even heard of.

Top row: Beautiful Zurich skyline; The twin towers of Grossmunster
Middle row: The Gates of Hell; Street scene in Zurich's old town
Bottom row: Me looking pensive in Zurich; Bridge spanning Lake Zurich

Chapter 4. Vaduz, Liechtenstein

Interesting fact: Liechtenstein is a Principality, meaning a prince rules it.

I wandered over to the man standing outside the yellow coach that belonged to the Liechtenstein Bus Company. I asked him whether it was due to depart anytime soon for Vaduz. He looked me up and down while taking a deep drag of his cigarette.

Five minutes previously, I'd arrived in the Swiss border town of Sargans after a pleasant, early morning train ride from Zurich. After buying a cup of coffee from the station cafe, I'd left the building and spotted the bus that would hopefully take me across the border to Vaduz, the capital of tiny Liechtenstein: the sixth smallest country in the world.

The man looked at the coffee in my hand. "Nein coffee!" he barked, shaking his head. He took another deep drag. "And I depart in ten minutes."

Bloody hell, I thought, I'd just met my first Liechten Swine.

2

Liechtenstein, sandwiched between Switzerland and Austria, is one of the richest nations on Earth. It makes a large proportion of its money from its sometimes questionable banking institutions and yet not many people have actually heard of the country, making it quite an elusive destination for the discerning tourist.

The border crossing went without incident and merely involved the bus traversing a gushing river (which I later found out was the Rhine). Soon after, we came to our first Liechtenstein town, Balzers, which featured an impressive stone castle built on top of a high hill. After seeing it, I had high hopes for Vaduz, because it too had a castle perched upon a high cliff side, and so sat back in my seat as we twisted and turned our way up through some decidedly Alpine countryside. One minute it was houses and farmland; the next, jagged and angry peaks appearing between thick layers of cloud. I fished out my thin guidebook and started reading.

3

Liechtenstein, I read, was a German-speaking country wholly contained within the Alps. Bizarrely, it was also the only German-speaking nation in the world not to have a border with Germany. Odder still is that Liechtenstein is famous for its manufacture of false teeth, and is the world's biggest manufacturer of sausage casings! Why didn't I know these facts before? I wondered. And had I ever eaten a sausage with a link to Liechtenstein?

For the next twenty minutes, we carried on upwards, slowing down the cars behind. But there was no angry beeping or lunatic swerving. Instead, everyone patiently waited for the bus to pull in at suitable sections so they could overtake. And then the bus came to a halt and everyone started getting off. At first, I thought it was a stop in the outskirts of Vaduz; when I was the only passenger left, and the driver turned around and gestured that I should depart, I realised we had arrived in the centre of the capital of Liechtenstein.

As the bus pulled away, I took a moment to take stock of my location. I was on the main road and there was a concrete bridge above my head. A church with a pointy spire was behind me. All of my fellow passengers were walking towards the bridge, but, instead of following them, I took out my map just as the first spatter of rain hit my face. I regarded the clouds. They were thick and grey. I fished the cap out from my rucksack and started walking towards the church.

4

The church turned out to be Vaduz Cathedral, a magnificent gothic structure with an impressively tall spire full of terrifying gargoyles all surrounding a colourful clock face. It looked like the tallest structure in the city, but then I concluded that calling Vaduz a city was like calling a fairy cake a gateau. With a population of just over 5000, it was more of a large village. But, like many a fairy cake, it was decidedly pretty: the cathedral in front of me proved this.

After managing to open its large wooden doors, I totally misjudged how heavy they were and the resulting clang when they bashed against their casings caused the few patrons inside to turn and stare. Luckily, there wasn't a service taking place, and so I smiled apologetically as the echoes receded. Inside was similar to many other churches I'd seen, and so, after only a cursory look around, I left, carefully closing the doors softly behind me. Just along from the cathedral was the Government Building of Liechtenstein; it featured an impressive coat of arms and some pointy turrets. A small tourist train was driving past it. It was making its way along the pedestrian-only Stadtle Street, packed mostly with Chinese tourists.

Chinese tourists, I was quickly discovering, were everywhere in Vaduz. Many of them were taking photos of each other in the most random of locations. One Chinese woman was snapping a photo of her daughter standing beside a standard-issue bench. Another woman was taking a photo of her kebab, and further along a man was attempting to take a snap of his wife jumping in mid-air. None of them seemed to mind the rain. I entered the Liechtenstein Centre, a tourist establishment selling all sorts of touristy things, the main draws being special Liechtenstein postage stamps and Liechtenstein passport stamps. The latter could be arranged for a few francs as a tourist memento. Though I considered the passport stamp a trite token, I queued up behind a Chinese couple and paid the three franc fee.

"My goodness," said the elderly woman in charge of the inkpad and stamp. "You have been to lots of places!" For a few seconds she had been flicking through my passport looking for a space for her Liechtenstein stamp. She stopped briefly at the visa for

Kazakhstan before moving onto the full-page visa sticker for Ethiopia.

"What was Ethiopia like?" she asked, her accent quite Germanic. "It is still as bad as it was?"

I shook my head. The Chinese couple were listening too; perhaps they were planning a trip there. "It's okay, actually. Quite nice; in fact, Addis Ababa has cafes and malls. I enjoyed myself there. So did my wife."

After a page had been duly adorned with an oval-shaped Liechtenstein stamp, I thanked the lady and resumed my sightseeing of Vaduz. When I stepped outside, I discovered the rain had stopped.

5

Stradtle Street was lined with bars and restaurants (including the kebab shop) and shops selling flags, cups, key rings and locally produced wines. I stopped opposite another building, this one the City Hall. It was arresting because of its higgledy-piggledy windows and flower-besieged archways. There was a large coat of arms stuck on the side with Vaduz written in capital letters. I looked at the trio of horse statues in front. They were popular with the Chinese contingent, all of whom were oohing and ahhing as they took thousands of pictures. For a fleeting moment, I wondered whether I should mount one of the statues and give my impression of Clint Eastwood (complete with whipping gestures), but then I pictured myself on YouTube and decided to move on.

After a kebab of my own, I decided to tackle a trail that led upwards towards Vaduz Castle, the most popular tourist site in the whole of Liechtenstein. Within seconds of stepping onto the cobbled path, I was panting like a rampant fiend. The gradient hadn't looked too bad when I'd spied it from between a couple of street-level restaurants, but, now that I was on it, the incline was hellish. Thankfully, at sections of the winding pathway there were wooden benches, which was just as well because I was in real danger of collapse.

I carried on for a few more minutes, but my pulse was racing out of control. The last thing I needed was to have a heart attack in Liechtenstein; instead of a pacemaker, I'd probably get some false teeth. I saw another bench and made a beeline for it, pretending, for the benefit of some fellow hikers, that I was stopping to look at my guidebook. As soon as they were out of earshot, I gulped air like a fat cod on a trawler deck.

Vaduz Castle was not actually open to the public; that much I knew, but I still wanted to see the official residence of Prince Hans Adam II, the sixth wealthiest leader in the world. As I resumed my trek, I thought about the Prince's two other titles, both far superior in my opinion. The Duke of Troppau sounded like someone who wouldn't stand any nonsense from his minions; the dastardly duke would dispatch his enemies with poison before seducing their beautiful wives. The Prince's other moniker was the even better sounding Count of Rierberg. This character sounded like an arch villain from an Agatha Christie novel; he would've almost certainly been a cad of the highest order.

Around a particularly bad bend, the trail led me to my prize. The twelfth-century structure, perched on the side of the mountain, was all turrets, towers and quite possibly torture chambers. It had red wooden shutters and a hefty wall surrounding it all. I imagined medieval archers taking aim through the dark gaps in the battlements, or guards dripping molten lead from the fortifications. The more I studied the stone structure, the more I realised it was exactly the type of castle I would want had I been a reigning monarch of a tiny Alpine country.

A couple of fifty-something hikers approached me. "Excuse me," asked the man in an American accent. "Do you speak English?"

I regarded the man and woman, all decked out in what looked like professional hiking apparel, including those silly stick things that seemed to have no discernible purpose apart from advertising the fact that a person was a *proper* walker. I nodded and told them I did, glancing at the woman's stick. It looked good for whacking pheasants and peasants. In my castle fantasy, I would have a gold-plated one. And I would whack someone every day with it.

"Great!" the man exclaimed excitedly. "Can you take a photo of us both, with the castle in the background?"

I nodded again and smiled. "No problem."

The couple huddled up as I pressed the button on their expensive camera. They seemed satisfied with the resulting image. "Where are you from?" the lady asked.

"England."

"England? Oh, we were there last week," she said. "In London. Loved every minute – apart from the weather. Boy does it rain a lot there. I don't know how you Brits put up with it." She noticed my wedding ring. "Is your wife with you?"

"No, I've murdered her and buried the body behind the castle," is what I almost said. Instead, I told them the truth: that Angela was at home in the UK and I was travelling alone.

"Alone? By yourself?" said the woman, taking a slight step closer to her husband. "Oh, my..." Both hikers looked at me as if I was insane. I smiled back, feeling slightly uncomfortable. The lady broke the silence. "Well, have fun, then. Thanks for taking the photo." She pulled her husband's arm and they shuffled up the hill.

I watched them go. Why was it so odd that I was travelling by myself? I thought. Did they think I was a serial killer or something? Surely people in the States sometimes travelled alone. I watched them for a moment longer and then turned around and walked down the hill in the opposite direction.

6

My last remaining sight of Vaduz was one that I almost didn't bother with, largely because it involved another hefty hike. My ankles and shins had been taking a real pounding over the last few days, and I was in two minds whether I could be bothered to walk there. But with nothing better to do, I decided to give it a go.

Ignoring the museums and crowds of central Vaduz, I headed away from the city centre towards an area known as Mitteldorf, a residential area full of quaint houses, vineyards, beautiful flowers and, amazingly, no tourists. Creepers crept adoringly over red and blue-painted houses, while bunches of crimson posies sat prettily along window ledges. Every building looked like it should have been in a painting or perhaps in a brochure for The Most Idyllic Village in the World.

I walked along a quiet lane, following a dry stone wall on one side, passing bunches of large green grapes on the other. In the distance, I could see the castle sitting on the side of its mountain, and, behind it, the peaks of the Alps. It was the best view of the castle I'd seen so far. The only worrying aspect of being in Mitteldorf was the absolute lack of people. Either everyone was at work or they were hiding from me. I turned towards a white house with blue shutters. Maybe I imagined it, but I was sure I saw the curtains rippling. After half an hour or so of aimless, but happy, wandering, I headed back into the centre.

7

I decided to seek out some Liechtenstein beer. It was easier said than done because none of the restaurants and bars seemed to sell it. I entered one of the tourist shops to ask an assistant for help.

"Liechtenstein beer?" answered the bemused teenage girl behind the counter. "I'm not sure Liechtenstein has its own beer...?"

I told the young woman that it did exist because I'd read about it in my guidebook. I showed her the page and she nodded uncertainly, and then suggested I try Cafe Wolf across the way. "If anyone has this beer, then they will."

And by God, she was right! The waiter in Cafe Wolf soon brought me a bottle of Brauhaus, Liechtenstein's finest (and only) ale. I was soon savouring its taste as I pondered my day trip to Vaduz.

It had turned out better than I'd expected it to be. True, there wasn't that much to do in Vaduz, but, for a country without an airport or even a train station, it wasn't doing too badly for itself. I looked up at the castle and smiled. Even in the clouds, it looked impressive: exactly my sort of castle. So far, it was winning in my 'Royal Abode' category.

Half an hour later, I was walking back to the bus stop, happy and content. After one more night in Zurich, it would be time for the next stop on my rapid travel through Europe: a small Mediterranean island with a distinctly British history.

Top row: The mightiness of Vaduz Castle – a proper castle, if you ask me; The city symbol on the side of the town hall
Middle row: Me wandering past the government building; Vaduz from above
Bottom row: Picture perfect prettiness in the Mitteldorf area of Vaduz; The spire of Vaduz Cathedral poking between some of the more modern elements of Liechtenstein

Chapter 5. Valletta, Malta

Interesting fact: Malta was the 48th happiest country in the world, according to a 2013 report, sandwiched cordially between Ecuador and Guatemala.

Air Malta delivered me into Luqa International Airport at just a few minutes before eight pm. After clearing passport control, I followed my fellow passengers towards the baggage carousels, passing billboard after billboard advertising casinos: *Dragonara Casino Experience! Got new slots!* one of them read. I carried on until I arrived at the luggage belts. And when it kicked into action, I was most gratified to find my bag was the first through the gates.

I was quickly in a taxi to the hotel, speeding along gleaming, bone-dry roads that fed into crisscross streets of the Maltese capital. My first impression of Valletta was one of *history*. The parched beige-white buildings, stately church domes and grand stone gateways (most of them dating from around the sixteenth century) all reeked of a glorious past. When British Prime Minister Benjamin Disraeli visited Malta in 1830, he called Valletta a 'city of palaces built by gentlemen for gentlemen'.

"Mr Smart," said the young lady behind the desk of the Grand Hotel Excelsior, "as you are an Elite Guest, you have been upgraded to the executive floor. You'll have a harbour view and ten percent off any spa treatments you may wish to have. In addition—"

"Elite Guest?" I interjected.

"Yes, sir..." she looked at her computer for a moment. "You have Elite status with... Expedia.com, the company you booked this hotel through." She looked up and smiled.

Wow! It had finally happened. After booking countless flights and hotels with Expedia, I'd hit the jackpot. Elite Guest status! I was a man with means; a man to be taken seriously: just one small step below an ambassador! I regained my composure and smiled back. "Thank you very much." I took the key card and marched off to the elevator like a lord.

The room was certainly better than the one I'd paid for. It even had a bottle of red wine with an envelope next to it: *With compliments*, it read. So this is how the other half lived, I mused, pouring myself a glass and sitting down at my executive desk, swivelling this way and that, checking again that the wine was actually free; it was, but then I wondered why I hadn't been upgraded in Zurich. I'd booked that hotel with Expedia, and also the ones in Oslo and Reykjavik. A quick Google search (with my executive-level free wi-fi) explained the reason why, and it made me smile and then grimace. I had achieved the Expedia Holy Grail of Elite Guest status because I'd spent a fortune with them: simple as that. They were repaying my loyalty by giving me upgrades in hotels that had signed up for the Elite Guest status scheme. The Grand Excelsior was one of them; none of the others were and none of the future ones would be either. But I could hardly complain – I was Elite in Malta!

2

I'd been to Malta once before. Many years previously, like many Brits, I went there as part of a package holiday with an ex-girlfriend. For close to two weeks, all we had done was sunbathe, drink and eat in cheap restaurants. Not once had we taken a trip to Malta's historic capital, Valletta, even though it had only been a short bus ride away, because we had deemed it too boring. But it was all different now: I was in the Maltese capital to bask in its glory, to bathe in its history and to sweat in its late July sunshine.

On my only full day in Malta, I swept open the expansive curtains to reveal my view of Valletta. As promised, it offered a panoramic view of an inviting Mediterranean Sea, with a collection of sand-coloured fort-like buildings sitting at the other side of a small but busy port. A flotilla of high-masted yachts was moored in a little harbour underneath them, overlooked by some expensive apartment blocks. In the water in front of the yachts, a gunmetal-grey coastguard vessel circled like a predatory shark. What it was looking for I couldn't guess, so I lowered my gaze to the pool area, which was largely deserted due to the relatively early hour. For a moment, I wondered whether I should jump into the elevator and rush over to an empty sun lounger to throw down a towel. Surely I deserved it, I thought. After all, I'd travelled to four countries already, and had eight more to go before I could have a break, and what better place to unwind for a few hours than in a hotel in which I enjoyed Elite status? No, I snapped at myself: rapid-fire travel across Western Europe did not allow for such luxuries, and, besides, I hated sunbathing. I turned from the window, picked up my guidebook and map, and headed out to see Valletta, the most southerly city I'd be visiting on my tour of Europe.

3

Even at half past eight in the morning, Malta was baking. But the sky was an almost perfect blue, contrasting with the elegant beige architecture around me. Every building was full of character, with high facades, dramatic windows and thin iron balconies. At one such window, a man in a white string shirt, with a cigarette dangling from his lip, was looking down at a passing car, hand rested on his chin. Opposite him, a buxom old woman with dyed red hair was pegging washing to a tiny line. Below them, a cat stretched out on the pavement, its body almost curving around the corner of one building.

I walked downhill along the northern coast road until I found myself overlooking a small and not yet open fish market. A couple of men were tending to some boats, but, apart from them, the place seemed deserted. I stopped to wipe my brow, braving a sneaky glance at the sun but regretting it immediately as spots blurred my vision: Malta was definitely the hottest country of my travels so far, and I rubbed my eyes as I took a deep slug of my water. I moved on again, this time turning inland, finding glorious shade from the tall buildings that lined the uphill avenue. I trekked upwards, passing small fruit-and-vegetable stores opening for the day, or women armed with sweeping brushes, flushing dust from doorways. At the top of the avenue, I turned right, up a series of steep steps, and then, just as I was starting to think I was the only tourist in Valletta, I saw everybody else.

4

Crowds of tourists were gawping at the upper reaches of St John's Co-Cathedral; others were sipping expensive coffees in the surrounding cafes. The 440-year-old cathedral (a co-cathedral due to the fact that the local Bishop shared it with another cathedral) was supposedly one of the world's greatest, but, to me, at least from the outside, it looked distinctly average. Scaffolding on some high places spoiled the effect further, and even its clock face and large wooden door could not make it any prettier. Even so, I walked around to the public entrance and paid my six euro fee to see its interior.

Inside was much better, full to bursting with glittering gold fresco masterpieces and people wandering around with handheld information speakers. I had one too, and pressed a number at random. A jaunty man's voice started telling me about a painting I had already passed, and so I stopped listening, looking at everything at top speed. The main reason I'd come into the cathedral had been to get onto the roof so I could see Valletta from above, but, after a few minutes of fruitless search, I was starting to give up. After passing an interesting skull on the wall, and then doing another quick circuit checking that I'd not missed any routes upwards, I decided to leave.

I joined my fellow tourists in a cafe opposite. Most of the accents were British, but a trio of men smoking cigarettes at the next table seemed to be locals. To me, the Maltese language sounded like a cross between Italian and French, with maybe a bit of Arabic thrown in for good measure. Written Maltese was unlike any of those, though, looking more like a strange fusion of Chinese and Icelandic. According to my guidebook, the Maltese phrase for 'What time is it?' read as 'X'hin hu', and the translation of 'Please' was 'Jekk joghabok'.

I opened a local English-language newspaper. Nothing much was happening in Malta, with only a story about Libya making the headlines. The Maltese government was wondering whether it was time to get their citizens out of Tripoli; things were hotting up there. Another story, about half way in, caught my interest, though. An American called Jeremiah Heaton had recently travelled to North Africa so he could trek to an uninhabited and extremely mountainous region called Bir Tawil. Astonishingly, it was an 800 square mile piece of Africa sandwiched between Egypt and Sudan that neither country had claimed. Knowing this, Jeremiah arrived, planted a homemade flag and declared himself king of North Sudan. He did this so his seven-year-old daughter could have her wish come true and become a real princess. Heaton hoped to gain recognition from both his neighbouring countries.

Along the horrendously busy Republic Street, the main tourist drag of the city, I came to a large open-air square bordered on one side by the mighty Grand Master's Palace, a tall, long flat-topped building that now housed the office of the Maltese President. People eating large ice-creams wandered past it, or else frolicked in the nearby fountains. I decided to buy an ice-cream myself, and with it, stood in a shaded corner of the square to regard the great palace.

The Grand Masters had not been chess champions, nor had they been hip-hop artists. In fact, they had been the leaders of the Knights Hospitallers, a military (but decidedly Christian) religious order who went around in the Middle Ages with large swords. Wearing scary black clothes with large white crosses emblazoned upon them, the Knights Hospitallers struck fear into any Muslim soldiers they came across due to their ferocious fighting methods. Oddly enough, though, the Hospitallers had actually started out as a relatively peaceful order of knights, caring for pilgrims on their way to and from the Holy Land. They worked in a field hospital in Jerusalem, thus the name, but eventually the order established themselves as a fighting force, and became such an asset to the Pope that he brokered a deal with the Spanish, whereby the knights could have sovereignty of Malta. The Spaniards agreed, but they did stipulate one thing: every year, the Knights Hospitallers had to send the Spanish king a Maltese falcon as a gift, which provided the name for a 1929 novel and subsequent film.

Apart from their work in the Middle East, the knights are most famous for their duty during the Great Siege of Malta in 1565. That was when they truly *earned* their place in Maltese history.

5

The Ottoman force was composed of almost two hundred vessels that contained 50,000 invaders. The ships were approaching the coast of Malta, hell-bent on taking the island and making it part of their ever-expanding empire. The Turkish commander, Suleiman the Magnificent, possessor of a great name, had personal issues with Malta. The previous year, the knights had captured his daughter's much-loved nurse, forcing her to become a slave. Suleiman vowed to 'wipe the Knights of Malta off the face of the earth'.

The Knights Hospitallers, led by Grand Master Jean de Valette, quickly assembled a force of around 6000 (most of them local men) and waited for the Ottomans to make landfall. While they did, a whole army of people pulled every crop from every field and picked every piece of fruit they could find, and then stored it away in secret troves. After collecting as much water as they could, they poisoned the island's wells and then they all hid themselves inside the various fortresses of Malta.

The Ottomans arrived at dawn in mid-May 1565 and wasted no time in blasting at the largest fortress, Fort St Elmo. Somehow, the defenders held on, getting supplies from boats making scud runs across the harbour, but, after a month of constant bombardment, the walls of St Elmo gave way and the Ottomans rushed in and hacked everyone to death. By the time the fort had been razed, over 1500 defenders lay dead, and to finish off the job, the Turks decapitated any knights they could find and racked up the bodies on makeshift wooden crucifixes that were sent out across the bay. In response, the Holy Knights chopped off the heads of every Turkish prisoner they had taken, loaded the heads into cannons and fired them back at the Ottoman camps. A clean siege it most certainly was not.

Inside the other forts, the defenders dug deep, knowing that the Ottomans were coming for them and would show no mercy. The Turks threw everything they had at the defenders. One hundred and thirty thousand cannon balls were fired at the Maltese fortifications, making it the most ferocious siege in history, but still the Knights would not capitulate. Queen Elizabeth I, awaiting news of the siege in England, famously stated that, if the Turks took Malta, the whole of Christendom was in peril because the rest of Europe was just on the doorstep for them.

By August, almost three months into the siege, the Ottomans had the breakthrough they so desperately needed. After a barrage of bombardment, they finally breached the walls of Fort St Michael and the defenders steeled themselves for a grisly battle. But then, instead of making good their breach, the Turks retreated, mistakenly believing that Christian forces from Sicily had just arrived on the island. When they found out they had been tricked, they tried to take the fort again, but with less gusto this time, especially as their retreat had allowed the knights precious time to rebuild their defences.

The problem was troop morale among the Turks. With the summer over, and no sign of the siege ending, the Ottoman forces had had enough. Many of them were succumbing to disease, and others were dying from wounds to which no one could attend. Without a steady supply of food and water, more men grew ill, but still, with their officers cajoling them into action, the Turks managed to mount a few half-hearted assaults until finally, in September, they gave up and headed back to their boats. The four-month Siege of Malta had ended, and Europe celebrated the last great battle of the Crusades.

Due to his leadership throughout the crisis, Grand Master Jean De Valette became a hero across the Christian world. So grateful were the various European leaders for his sending the Muslims packing that they sent piles of cash to Malta, which Valette used to build a grand walled city to rival any in the world, a city that would be named after himself: Valletta.

6

I continued with my walk, passing a few red telephone boxes that looked distinctly British. Unlike their graffiti-covered UK counterparts, these ones were all clean and well cared for; even better than that, they seemed to be in full working order. Further on, I spied a kiosk that proudly stated it sold 'Today's London newspapers'. A collection of Daily Mirrors and Daily Expresses sat in the display mesh.

The strong link between Malta and Britain dates from 1814 when Britain expelled the hugely unpopular French. For the British, gaining Malta provided them with a strategic stopping point for their navy, a link between Europe and North Africa: so strategic, in fact, that the British decided to stay put. Even after independence in 1964, the connection between both countries remains, thanks in no small part to the half a million UK holidaymakers taking their summer vacations on the islands.

Another distinctly British institution in Valletta is a bar called, rather unimaginatively, *The Pub*. It was just around the corner from the Grand Master's Palace; it looked small from the outside and even smaller from the inside. Capable of holding just 24 seated guests, the darkened rectangular room was already two-thirds full, and, as I walked to the bar, I caught snippets of English conversation, mainly about the weather. As I ordered my pint of Cisk from the Brit behind the bar, I took in the decor. The Pub was a proper British hostelry, right down to the British flags draped across the ceiling, foreign money pasted around the bar area and the John Smiths Bitter on tap. "Here you go, mate," said the barman. "A pint of Malta's finest."

I sat in the only remaining seating area, by the door. On the wall was a placard containing a newspaper article about the late Oliver Reed. The actor had been filming scenes from *Gladiator* in Valletta, and, during a break in his schedule, had decided to pop into The Pub for an afternoon tipple. After downing a few drinks (which, according to some reports, amounted to eight pints of lager, a dozen rums and half a bottle of whisky), Reed suddenly keeled over. He died on the way to hospital of a massive heart attack. But what a way to go.

"Waiting for your better half to finish shopping?" asked the man at the next table. Like me, he was by himself, nursing an almost empty pint of beer. He looked to be in his late-fifties and had a considerable beer-assisted belly flopped out in front of him. His accent suggested an Essex heritage.

"Actually, no," I replied. "I'm in Malta by myself."

The man threw me a look, similar to the one the American lady had given me in Vaduz.

"My wife's back in England," I explained. "But she is meeting me...," I mentally calculated when, "in about a week and a half."

"So you're in Malta on holiday by yourself?" He scrunched his face, suggesting that this was not a normal thing to do. "By the way, I'm Graham."

I shook his hand and introduced myself. "No, I'm not on holiday, really, and I'm only here for one full day. I'm flying to France tomorrow, then Brussels a few days after that. I'm meeting my wife in Copenhagen."

Graham picked up his drink and took a hearty swig. "Brussels? Copenhagen? What are you, an airline pilot or something?"

I decided to tell him the truth: I was on a mission to visit as many Western European countries as I could, and that Malta was only one of the many stops on the trip. "By the end, if everything goes according to plan, I should have been to twenty-two countries."

Graham whistled. "Twenty-two? I didn't know there were that many." Suddenly, an electronic beep sounded. It was Graham's phone. "The wife has just texted," he told me. "Time to go for me. She's finished her shopping and I'm meeting her in that square around the corner." He stood up and we shook hands. "But nice meeting you, Jason. And good luck with the rest of your trip. It sounds...umm..."

"—Fun?"

"I was going to say, torture, actually. Twenty-odd countries, all for a day or two at a time: it sounds like my idea of hell. Give me a sun-lounger and a nice bar any day. Each to their own, though. Take care now." He headed for the bright sunshine beyond the door.

7

Half an hour later, I was ambling along one of Valletta's main shopping streets, lined with green streamers and dangling red and gold banners. The tourist shops were doing a busy trade, especially with window shoppers, I noticed. A couple of teenage girls in tiny shorts were buying large ice-creams while a squat man in a dark business suit meandered his way through a collection of slow-moving pensioners. I was doing the same thing, but in the opposite direction, where thankfully the crowds thinned as I made my way downhill. At the bottom, overlooking the sea, was the Siege Bell Memorial.

A set of steps led up to a columned temple that contained the bell, and a young couple were posing on them, taking photos of themselves. After they had finished, I climbed past them to stare at the massive bell, placed there as a reminder of what had happened in Malta during the Second World War. *This bell tolls in memory to those who gave their lives during the Siege of Malta 1940 – 1943*, a metal placard read.

This more modern Siege of Malta was one of the most fiercely contested battle arenas of the Second World War. In fact, the dockyards of Valletta suffered from one of the heaviest aerial bombing raids in the history of warfare. Rather like the Ottomans centuries before, the Germans and Italians recognised that Malta held strategic importance in Southern Europe, and, so in an attempt to break the islanders, three thousand bombing missions were carried out, but, like the historic Knights Hospitallers before them, the people of Malta would not surrender. Such was their resistance that the Axis powers gave up and diverted their attention to Tunisia instead.

I took a photo of the placard and bell, and then crossed the road to have a walk through the Lower Barrakka Gardens, a peaceful place of palm trees, fountains and memorials. The largest monument looked like a Roman temple, but was actually only around two hundred years old. It was dedicated to a great British admiral called Alexander Ball, a man universally adored in Malta thanks to his handling of the expulsion of the French in 1800. I walked to a terrace overlooking the harbour, took a few photos and then sat down in a busy outdoor cafe to have a cooling drink. Though it was hot and humid, I was glad with my lot in life.

Valletta had proved itself a great little city, full of life and vitality. And later that evening, as I ate a meal in a restaurant overlooking the harbour, I thought about how lucky I was to be able to travel to many beautiful places. I watched a boat crossing from left to right, thinking of the next country on my journey through Europe: Monaco, the second-smallest nation in the world.

Top row: The historic buildings of Valletta; English phone boxes are a fixture of Valletta
Middle row: The Pub – where Oliver Reed had his final drink; Busy street in Valletta
Bottom row: Lower Barrakka Gardens; Me standing in front of the Siege Bell

Chapter 6. Monaco

Interesting fact: Monaco has the second smallest railway system in the world, after the Vatican.

After a brief transit through Rome, I arrived in Nice, southern France. As a child, I'd loved the name Nice, unaware that I'd been mispronouncing it, thinking it was amazing that a town could be named after such a lacklustre adjective and a brand of biscuit. The sugarcoated rectangular treat, with the cute little rounded perforations around the edge, was a mainstay of the Smart household when I'd been growing up.

Nice seemed very pretty, but I was not in France to see its fifth most populous city, I was in Nice because of its proximity to Monaco, the second-smallest country in the world. Monaco didn't have its own airport (though it did have a few helipads) and so getting to it would involve a twenty-two minute train ride. That said, I couldn't help but be impressed with Nice as the airport bus travelled alongside the city's long and pebbly-beached promenade, full to bursting with tanned bodies and roller-skaters. The sea looked inviting – a lustrous blue, busy with bobbing heads and nervous paddlers.

My hotel was nowhere near the beach: it was close to the main train station, along a busy street full of cafes, clothes shops and groups of teenage punks wearing studs, nose rings, ripped black tights and shocks of green and red hair. I dragged my suitcase along the wide tram tracks and settled down in the hotel for the night.

2

Monaco, like Liechtenstein and Andorra, is a principality. The current ruler, Prince Albert II, is the son of American actress Grace Kelly, who was married to the prince's father, Prince Rainier II. Even though France surrounds Monaco (apart from its coastline on the Mediterranean), the two nations have been friendly, with the only real spat occurring in 1963, when French president Charles de Gaulle decided to blockade Monaco over its sometimes lax banking and tax laws. He was incensed that wealthy French citizens had been welcomed into Monaco to become tax exiles there.

My journey to Monaco began at Gare de Nice Ville, Nice's main train station. As it was a sunny Friday, the station was full of tourists trying to buy tickets from automatic machines that only offered occasional glimpses of English. Most people gave up and joined the horrendous queue to buy a ticket from an actual person. Not me, though; I persevered and, once I'd managed to procure a ticket, made my way to the overcrowded platform to wait.

As usual, the train arrived at another platform, which meant a mad dash to reach the train on time. In the end, I needn't have bothered rushing: the train wasn't going anywhere for a while. Crowds of people were battling by the doors, reminding me of how trains were boarded in India.

I joined one mob and fought my way inside the hot and sweaty carriage, finding myself sandwiched between a Chinese man and a young German woman wearing a huge backpack. Over the course of the next thirty minutes, I would do battle with the backpack, but for now I attempted to manoeuvre myself into the least cramp-inducing position possible while trying to ignore the fact that I was almost nose-to-nose with an old man opposite who seemed to have a permanent grin.

The doors closed and then opened again. A woman was trying to gain entry into the carriage. "There's no room in here, lady," said an American woman's voice. "We can hardly breathe as it is." The newcomer looked and saw that the American was correct. She stepped back and the doors closed once more.

The journey to Monaco was mercifully quick, but, because I wasn't anywhere near a window, all I saw was a white bulkhead. And people. The German girl's backpack had dug into my back and neck the whole way, and at one point had almost knocked me into the Chinese guy. Defiantly, I'd thrust out my shoulders and arched my back in an attempt to thwart the backpack, but it pushed back in equal measure and so I'd given up, broken and weary. When we eventually stopped and the doors opened at Gare de Monaco, I emerged from the train red and sweating.

3

Even from just outside the train station, I could see that Monaco was a beauty: a place of expensive high-rise apartments, jagged mountain peaks and endless palm trees. It also had a large harbour full of large white yachts, which was where I was headed first. I passed an outdoor cafe, where the smell ranged from expensive perfume to Cuban cigars. Monaco was a city of wealth. From Formula One racing drivers to James Bond actors, Monaco attracted an elite crowd.

Port Hercule is home to hundreds of yachts and other expensive vessels; they were everywhere, moored up like trophies. Across the other side of the harbour was the old town of Monaco-Ville, known locally as *Le Rocher*. Perched on the top of a rocky outcrop was the *Palais Princier*, a place I would be visiting later on. For now, though, I took in the panoramic view of downtown Monaco and then set off to see if I could locate the tourist information centre.

I rounded a bend, passing a McLaren supercar parked by the side of the road; further on, a Rolls Royce sat idling in a parking bay, and, from around a hairpin bend, the deep roar of a Ferrari was coming my way: three high-end cars in less than two minutes. I tried to peer into the Ferrari's window to see if it was anyone famous, but it was gone too quickly for me to see. I'd not seen such a wealth of supercars anywhere else in the world, and that included places like Doha and Dubai.

Away from the harbour, Monaco was hilly, and not particularly well signposted. I followed a series of steps until I realised I was lost. Sweat was bubbling on my head, trickling down my back and chest, and so I found a bus stop to rest in. The arrival of an elderly woman, who gave me the once-over, and a disdainful one at that, soon had me on my way, blundering along a street until I came to a set of steps. At the top, I found myself on Boulevard de la Republique, a quaint little street made up of estate agents, beauty shops and small cafes. Not unexpectedly, I couldn't find the street on my map, and so I wandered around for a good fifteen minutes, until I retraced my steps and found the tourist information centre. It seemed rather small and dark inside, but, when I pulled on the door, it opened freely and I entered its blissfully air-conditioned interior.

"Bonjour!" said the young woman behind the desk, "Ca va?"

I gave my stock phrase. "Bonjour! Parlez-vouz Anglais?"

The woman nodded. "Of course." If she noticed the sweat patches on my shirt, she didn't give any indication.

I asked her about getting my passport stamped, which brought a look of confusion, but then she seemed to realise something.

"I think you mean the Monaco passport stamp?"

I nodded.

"Then you must go to Monaco. This is a French tourist information centre. You are in France, monsieur!"

I opened my mouth and then closed it again.

The woman smiled. "Do not worry; you are only a few minutes away from the Monaco tourist information centre. Look, I will show you." She produced a tourist map, and circled where we were, then explained how to get back to Monaco. "Just walk left from here, around this bend, and then take the stairs down the hill. The tourist centre is just there."

It didn't seem far at all, and I thanked the woman for her assistance. With my new map, I left the French tourist information centre and headed back to the border.

The France-Monaco border was just another pretty little side street. Nothing indicated it was the boundary that separated two nations, apart from the marking on my new map. I waited for a woman carrying a bag full of apples and baguettes to cross the border, and then stood in the middle of a pathway and aimed the camera at myself. In all my travels, across more than one hundred countries, I had never taken a photo of myself straddling a border, until now. Job done, I headed down some steep steps and found myself outside the Monaco Tourist Information Centre, a much larger affair than its French counterpart. Inside was an equally friendly young woman, who, unlike the lady in the Liechtenstein tourist office, stamped my passport for free. Job number two done, and so I found a nice little park tucked away behind the office and took a rest on a bench.

A crowd of Chinese tourists came through the park, all of them stopping by a large pond in order to take some photos of a metal lizard spewing water from its mouth. One man tried to get closer to it and stepped onto the forbidden grass. A large sign warned people not to do this, and I looked around, waiting for some official to apprehend him. No one did, and the man returned to his group unscathed.

He was lucky, though, because Monaco was full of police officers and peppered with numerous CCTV cameras. I couldn't remember seeing so many cameras trained upon the streets of any city I'd been to, but now realised why it was safe to park a Lamborghini outside a supermarket and not risk it being damaged or stolen.

It was time to move on. After studying my map, I plotted my route to Place du Casino, which turned out to be just around the corner in an area of Monaco called Monte Carlo. I'd always assumed that Monte Carlo was the capital of Monaco, whereas, in actual fact, it was just the most famous district of the country, due to the casino called after it.

One side of Place du Casino was taken up by the impossibly posh looking Hotel de Paris. It featured fanciful domes, expensive facades and sweeping balconies, and charged over a thousand euros per night for a sea-view room. The main draw of Place du Casino, however, was the country's largest gambling arena – the mighty Monte Carlo Casino, a large and majestic cream-yellow building that had a selection of supercars parked outside. The bright red Ferrari was attracting the most attention until a gleaming and impossibly silver Bentley cruised past, the woman in the passenger seat all lip gloss and dark sunglasses. The car looked like it was coated in chrome, a design I'd never seen on a car before. Fifty pairs of eyes watched as it made its way around the roundabout.

5

Monaco's hugely successful foray into the world of organised gambling came about because the country needed an injection of cash. The Grimaldi ruling house was on the verge of bankruptcy, largely due to some sections of the tiny country breaking away and then not paying any taxes; to bolster the coffers, someone came up with the idea of building a casino. Someone else pointed out that if they did, then they would also need a direct train line to Paris to get people to come, and then they would have to build a few hotels to cater for them. With the plans finalised, and budgets arranged, construction started on the casino complex in 1858; five years later, it was complete. All they had to do now was come up with a name for it.

Originally, the casino was to be named Spelugues, but someone decided that this was an ugly moniker, and so it was named Monte Carlo (Mount Charles) after the then-ruling prince of Monaco. Almost as soon as it opened its large doors, the casino became a hit, with people spending their money like there was no tomorrow. In no time at all, the casino was making so much money that the Grimaldis abolished taxation for all their citizens.

I walked past the entrance of the casino, walking along a street with cafes and a small shopping mall along one side. I followed the map and then stopped, immediately recognising the sight in front of me. The tight bend in the road was part of the Monaco Grand Prix circuit, a section known as the Fairmont Hairpin. In my twenties, I watched countless battles between Michael Schumacher and Damon Hill on this very bend, and it was strange to be staring right at it, instead of watching it on a television screen. An open-topped tourist bus snaked its way around the bend and I decided to go for some lunch.

6

I chose a cafe overlooking the harbour for the simple reason that it advertised it sold local San Marino beer. I sat down at the rear and ordered one. It came a few minutes later and tasted great, mainly because it was so cold and I was so hot. I ordered some food too, a simple cheeseburger. As I looked over some photos I'd taken, I could hear the unmistakable sound of a baby crying.

A middle-aged couple were sitting at the next table to me, closer to the baby. Both looked wealthy and well-to-do, him with a Rolex watch, her with some expensive jewellery dangling from her neck and wrist. After a particularly incessant discord of infant wailing, she tutted, causing the mother of the baby to turn around. The posh lady turned to her husband, her American voice completely audible. "I hope they're not staying here for long. It shouldn't be allowed. It's like that baby in First Class all over again. Crying all the way over from New York."

I smiled to myself. The uber-rich always thought they were a cut above everybody else, but, twenty minutes later, when my bill came, I felt like being pompous myself. *How bloody much?* I looked at the bill again: twenty-seven euros! *Twenty-seven!* The small bottle of San Marino alone was nine euros. It was just like Oslo. Western Europe was draining me of money. I paid up, left the cafe and headed up a snaking pathway towards the old town.

7

At the top of the hill was an enchantingly pretty square. There was a historic palace, a statue of a furtive man dressed as a monk, a cobbled square and a set of medieval buildings. The largest building, the Prince's palace, was the official residence of Albert II, but, unlike the vast majority of royal palaces across Europe, the Grimaldi family had lived in it for centuries without moving anywhere else. I wandered over to the statue. It was of Francesco Grimaldi, who in 1297 had dressed as a monk to gain entry into Monaco castle. When he had done so, he ushered his own troops through the entrance so they could take it. This act made him the first member of the House of Grimaldi to reign over Monaco. He didn't last long, though, because four years later, the Genoese threw him out.

The palace was an odd-looking thing: a jigsaw of styles and architecture put together seemingly at random. The left-hand side seemed normal enough, cream-coloured and full of square windows, but over on the right was the odd-looking side. It looked like builders had added a grey stone castle to the end, with turrets and thin, arch-shaped windows.

Behind the palace was a series of jagged grey cliffs, once impenetrable to enemy attack, but now an arresting sight for the tourist invaders of the old town. In front of the palace was a sentry box with a white-uniformed soldier. I watched him have a little wander around when suddenly a whistle reverberated over the cobbles and I turned to see a policeman ordering tourists to move to the side. Many were ambling along in the middle of the road that led around the edge of the courtyard, oblivious. His colleague, standing a little further along, was whistling and gesturing too, until eventually they had everybody, including me, standing at the side. Then the reason became clear: two black Lexus limousines were emerging from the palace. Everyone strained to see, and, in one of them with the number plate MC01, there he was – Prince Albert himself – sitting in the back. I barely had time to register his presence before both cars exited the courtyard. Seeing Prince Albert of Monaco would, as it turned out, be my only flirtation with European royalty on the whole trip.

8

Away from the palace, a few streets led eastwards. The one I chose was full of ice-cream parlours, souvenir shops and overpriced cafes. Tourists packed them. Above the crowds, however, was a glimpse of what it must have been like in pre-casino Monaco: wrought iron street lamps, wooden shutters and pastel-coloured four-storey buildings with plant-pot-laden verandas. I could only guess at what the people who lived in these fine buildings thought of the never-ending parade of French, Italian, Chinese and American voices cascading below their quarters. An elbow shove brought me back to street level, and so I ambled aimlessly until I arrived outside Monaco Cathedral, a massive grey building that was taller than everything else around and yet was so tightly packed into the jumble of the old town that I only found it by chance. In 1956, Prince Albert's father had married Grace Kelly inside the cathedral. Both are now buried there.

"Hat off, please," said a man inside the cathedral. He wasn't speaking to me, but to a pair of young American tourists, but, since I had a hat on, I removed mine. I looked for somewhere to pay an entrance fee, but was gratified to find there wasn't one. I followed the large white arrow into the nave.

There were not many people inside, just a couple of pensioners sitting on the wooden pews, and a few Chinese tourists at the front, staring at the altar. The Americans wandered just ahead of me, pausing at the first statue and then at some stained glass windows. I skipped past them, staring at the floor. Along the edge of the pews were the tombs of Monaco's past rulers, but I didn't stop until I found the one I was looking for – the only one with vases of flowers laid upon it; the inscription read *Gratia Patricia*, after Grace Patricia Kelly, the Princess of Monaco. She had died in 1982, aged 52, after suffering a stroke that caused her to drive her car down a mountainside. Her husband, Prince Rainier never got over the loss, took up chain-smoking and eventually died in 2005. He was buried next to his wife.

9

I looked at my watch and realised it was time to leave. I had a train back to Nice to catch. As I wandered back down the hill, once more savouring the panoramic views of the harbour and all its glamour, I nodded in silent appreciation at Monaco. It was a great little country, perhaps the best of all the micro-states I'd visited so far. It had an excitement about it, a side that made the blood flow. Even the 9-euro bottle of beer (which would turn out to be the second-most expensive drink on my whole trip) had not dampened my enthusiasm for the place. Monaco, from the tiny observations I'd made, was definitely a contender for my favourite place in Western Europe so far.

Top row: The amazing harbour and skyline of Monaco (with Italy in the background); Statue of Francesco Grimaldi
Middle row: Monaco Cathedral, which contains the tomb of Grace Kelly; Monte Carlo Casino – a major money spinner for the country
Bottom row: A famous hairpin bend from the Formula 1 track; The Prince's Palace

Chapter 7.Brussels, Belgium

Interesting fact: Brussels Airport sells more chocolate than any other single place on Earth.

Belgium annoyed me before I even stepped foot inside its chocolate-filled airport. A baggage handlers' strike meant my arrival from Nice into Brussels International was a scene of utter chaos. People everywhere were walking this way and that, their facial expressions a mixture of bewilderment and anger. Others were standing next to redundant carousels, waiting for movement that would never start. A few proactive passengers were besieging people in yellow high-visibility jackets.

As a veteran of air travel, I knew exactly where I needed to be, but the already mile-long queue at the baggage reclaim desk made me rethink my options. With every newly arriving group of passengers facing the same situation, I quickly concluded that I was not going to see my suitcase that night, but neither was I going to stand in this queue for the next five hours. Instead, I switched on my phone and filled in an online lost baggage form. I pressed 'send' and took the escalator into the bowels of the airport to the train platforms. Half an hour later, I was in the centre of Brussels.

It was actually quite liberating being able to walk to my hotel without the hindrance of a suitcase lagging behind me. Besides, in my small backpack I had enough essentials to keep me going: my netbook, adapter plugs, a spare pair of socks and underwear (something I'd done since once losing a suitcase in Tallinn), and my guidebook were all with me. It was only after I'd checked into the hotel that I discovered I had no toothbrush, deodorant or shampoo. Oh well, I thought, things could have been much worse.

I went out to find something to eat. Being in Belgium meant things were not cheap, even in a fast-food burger joint. Afterwards, I walked along a darkening street of downtown Brussels, passing a few waffle shops and chocolate displays, when I spotted a small convenience store. It would suffice for the missing essentials from my suitcase. After a quick look inside, I found everything except for the toothbrush. I went up to the counter and asked the flabby man sitting at the till if he spoke English.

"Non," he replied bluntly. He looked down at his newspaper.

Charming. I didn't know the French word for toothbrush, or even the word for tooth, so I coughed instead, which made him look up. I mimed brushing my teeth.

The man said nothing.

"Je voudrais," I said, "une...toothbrush."

"Eh?"

I pointed to my teeth. "Une toothbrush, sil vous plais." I mimed the brushing action again.

The man looked nonplussed. I wondered whether he was a simpleton, because I was pretty sure that if I saw someone miming that particular motion, and they were doing it in a shop that maybe sold toothbrushes, I'd know what they wanted.

A woman standing behind me said something to the shopkeeper. He replied to her gruffly and then sighed. He huffed further as he hoisted his fat arse from his chair and wandered down one of his aisles. He came back with a toothbrush and placed it with my other items. Transaction complete, I left the shop and returned to my hotel.

2

The next morning was cold and drizzly, a typical day in Northern Europe. I didn't care, though, because I was standing in the centre of the Grand Place, Brussels' most famous and deliciously beguiling attraction. All around the edge of the large square were ornately decorated palaces, glittering halls and fetching guild houses, their designs incorporating golden statues, misshapen gargoyles and intricately patterned columns and archways. It was no wonder that, in 2010, the Grand Place had been voted Europe's most beautiful square, even beating such luminaries as Red Square and Trafalgar Square.

The tallest building in Grand Place is the town hall. Its 310ft spire looked like it was made from bone china and might topple with only the slightest gust of wind. But it had stood proudly for over five hundred years. I gazed at the statues embedded in the walls, and then slowly turned 360 degrees to take in the majesty all around. Grand Place really was the jewel in Brussels' crown.

Because I was there so early, a couple of vans and wagons littered the square, most of them unloading provisions into the pricy cafes that would be full to capacity later on. In the middle of the square, a flower market was being set up. Just along from it stood a group of Japanese tourists, all wearing earpieces as they listened to their guide. They stood looking at a large building known as the Bread House, named so because it had once been a bread market.

As for me, after one last look at the buildings in the Grand Place, I decided it was time to see Brussels' second most famous attraction, Manneken Pis.

3

Manneken Pis is a small bronze statue of a little boy urinating. The almost four-hundred-year old figure stands on a nondescript street corner above a small basin. Except it does not. The original sits inside the Bread House, as it has done since 1965. The one I was staring at was about fifty years old.

I looked at the boy. He was leaning back as he took aim into the small pool of water below him. A steady stream of trickling water tumbled from his minute metal penis. To protect him from greedy hands, the naked boy was behind a wrought iron fence. He was small, just a smidgeon over 60cm tall, but the sculptor had done a good job of creating the illusion of a full head of hair on the boy, as well as an expression of brazen cheekiness.

A dozen Indian tourists had got there before me and were crowding around the fence, taking photos of one another in front of the bronze boy. I waited for them to finish but they were taking ages. In the end, I simply manoeuvred my way to the front, wondering why it had become so famous. After all, it was hardly the best statue in the world. Also, its history is a little sketchy.

In one account, the sculpture is a memorial to a boy with a keen pair of eyes. Noticing spies planting explosives around his city, the boy had urinated over the smouldering wicks. Another, more elaborate reason for the statue involved someone called Duke Godfrey III.

Even though the Duke was only two years old, he had a considerable number of enemies, all of whom wished him great harm so they could take over his dukedom. As a battle raged between the Duke's soldiers and their enemies, someone placed the infant's cradle high in a tree branch. When the Duke's men secured their decisive victory, young Godfrey precariously stood up and peed over his fallen foes. But, even with these two outlandish explanations, no one knows the real the reason why the extravagantly named Brussels sculptor, Hieronimus Duquesnoy, decided to make the statue.

Bizarrely, the statue has been stolen seven times. The first theft occurred in 1695. It was later discovered, thankfully intact, on the steps of a brothel.

The next heist occurred in 1817, and the statue was discovered a short while later, broken up into several pieces. After a brief investigation, the thief was arrested and, such was the uproar about the vandalism, he was sentenced to twenty years in prison.

The most recent disappearance of Manneken Pis was in the 1960s when a group of students stole the statue, which prompted its move to the Bread House. I snapped a photo of the little fellow, almost being elbowed out of the way by the Indian tourists as I did so, and then left for pastures new.

4

I'd been to Belgium once before. As a university student in the late 80s, a group of us had decided it would be a great idea to drive through the Channel Tunnel and stay in France for a few days. Our plan had been to drive to the German border, but the furthest we got was Boulogne. We did do a side trip to the Belgian border town of Veurne, though.

Veurne turned out to be interesting for two reasons. The first was because of an incident inside a small grocer's shop. I'd drawn the short straw and had been sent in to buy provisions. As I traipsed around the aisles, I could see the proprietor – a middle-aged man with a keen eye – studying me. To be fair, I'd have done the same thing because I did look like someone to keep an eye on. I was dressed scruffily in a weather-beaten coat, I had bleary eyes from lack of sleep, and my look was finished with a few days' growth of student stubble.

I found a cheap pack of ham in the cold section and picked it up. I did the same with a loaf of bread and then walked to the counter, the man eyeing me all the while. After I laid my items down, the man shook his head. "Non!" he said sharply, pointing at my coat with interest. He prodded my chest, as if expecting contraband to fall out. When nothing did, he prodded me again.

"Stop it," I said, but he wouldn't and was now also shouting at me in rapid-fire French. I decided the man was insane and so fled the shop without my items.

The second thing occurred at lunchtime. Because of the shop debacle, we decided to go to a cafe for lunch. Three of us ordered poulet et fritte, but my friend Jon ordered a prawn salad because, strangely, it was the cheapest thing on the menu. When Jon's plate arrived, he was horrified to see that the prawns had not been shelled. Five or six of the spindly beasts were lying on a bed of lettuce and tomatoes.

"What do I do with these?" he asked.

Before I could say anything, Phil, a maths student who later trained to be a teacher with me, decided to have some fun. "You just eat them," he stated calmly, cutting into his chicken with an air of nonchalance. "Down the hatch."

Jon looked doubtful, but then examined one of the prawns. He picked it up with his fingers and peered at the legs and then the head. He shook his own head. "There's no way you just eat all that."

"That's how you do it," said Phil. "The way posh people do it, anyway."

Jon still looked uncertain but Phil's nonchalance was giving him pause for thought, as was the air of indifference Tony and I were feigning. Jon regarded the prawn again. We all waited for his decision. It was hard to keep a straight face. "And people eat the feelers and eyes?" Jon asked.

"Yeah," said Phil. "The eyes are supposed to be the best bit...the delicacy."

Jon shrugged and bit the head off and began crunching away. The rest of us held our breaths, caught between an outburst of hilarious laughter and vomit-induced nausea.

"Not bad," he announced. "A bit crunchy, but...tasty." He snapped off a leg and began munching away on that too. Only then did we burst into laughter.

5

Not far from Manneken Pis was a large mural of Tintin. The boy with the famous quiff had been painted climbing down a fire escape with his two faithful sidekicks: Snowy the dog and the excellently named Captain Haddock. All were life-sized and in full colour.

Tintin is big business in Belgium. To date, his comic strips (created by Belgian artist, Georges Remi) have sold more than 200 million copies and have been translated into seventy languages.

Charles de Gaulle once famously said that his only international rival was Tintin. After a final glance at the huge cartoon, I left the boy behind and headed along Rue de l'Etuve, a long straight thoroughfare filled with chocolatiers, restaurants and tourists shops, until I arrived at a small park.

The park was small but it did have a bench. I sat on it and studied my map just as a Chinese family arrived: Dad, Mum and a sullen-looking son aged about fifteen. Dad made a beeline for some giant plant pots. The pots were taller than a person and full to the brim with bedding plants. Dad said something and Mum quickly moved into position in front of one of the pots. The teenager looked less ecstatic, but slowly shuffled to the side of his mother, rolling his eyes and sighing. Dad moved back with his expensive camera and waved his son to move closer towards his mum. After an audible sigh, the teenager stood closer to his mother, balefully glancing at me to see if I was watching. He saw that I was and so sighed again. Dad pressed the button of his camera but when he checked the resulting image, he didn't look happy and began shouting at his errant son, making them pose again. This time, instead of sighing, the boy forced a smile. A great memento of a day out in Brussels, I thought.

My phone rang. It was a number I didn't recognise and when I answered, a male voice spoke to me in French. Eventually he switched to English and explained that he worked at Brussels Airport and that my luggage had been found. He wanted to confirm that I was still in Brussels before sending it to my hotel. When I told him I was, he sounded relieved. "This is good news for me. A lot of baggage has gone to people who have already left the city. So that is why I check with you first. Someone will drop it off this afternoon. Thanks for staying in Brussels."

The call ended, and I decided to find the sister statue of Manneken Pis. I started a stroll through quaint alleyways full of tempting smells of chocolate and waffles. Chocolatiers were everywhere in Brussels, their window displays full of exquisitely packaged confectionery to entice the sweet-toothed browser. I ignored them until I found Jeanneke Pis, the statue of the little girl, hidden along a tight alleyway that formed the rear entrance to a few restaurants. The small metal girl with pigtails was squatting down behind a metal grille as water trickled from her nether regions into the basin below. It wasn't quite as good as the boy I'd seen earlier, and was much younger, dating from 1987, but I still leaned in to take a photo. As I did, a waiter from one of the restaurants came out of the door and lit a cigarette. He watched me take the photo, which made me feel self-conscious, and so I decided to leave. Besides, it was time to head into Brussels' underground for a train journey. I wanted to see the Atomium.

6

The Atomium looked decidedly odd. The gigantic stainless steel spheres in front of me were connected by massive metal tubes that towered above the landscape. It resembled some sort of alien condominium. What it actually represented though was the arrangement of atoms in iron. And it wasn't that modern either – it dated from the 1950s.

Parties of school children were snaking through the park towards the Atomium with me, their stressed teachers harrying them to hurry up, to move to one side or to simply stop pushing each other. Another large group of Chinese tourists was also in attendance, most of them posing in large gaggles with the Atomium behind them. I passed them all and joined the queue to buy a ticket to go inside the elevator. With a rush of air we ascended, speeding towards the highest of the eight spheres. When the lift disgorged us into a circular viewing area, I rushed towards one window, beating the Chinese stampede, to eagerly take in the view. I really should've chosen my moment with more care, though: with a layer of cloud and a fine drizzle in the air, the view was not great. My phone rang. It was Angela. She asked me where I was.

"In the Atomium."

There was a pause. "I won't ask. I'm ringing to check that everything's okay for Thursday."

"Everything's fine. I'm going to Luxembourg tomorrow, and then I get the train to Amsterdam the day after to meet the boys. Then Copenhagen to meet you. I'll be there an hour before you so I'll just wait in the airport."

"Okay, that sounds fine. Oh, have you got your suitcase back?"

"It's on its way right now."

"Good. Well, I'll see you on Thursday, then. You can buy me a Danish pastry while you wait."

7

Back in the centre of Brussels, I made my way up a slight gradient to what I hoped was the Royal Palace. I passed a great little park, full of tulips and statues, and was so taken by them that I tripped over a pavement. I didn't fall, but my cartoonish stumble and cart-wheeling arms made a woman walking nearby look over.

The palace was enormous, stretching out across the whole street. It reminded me of Buckingham Palace, especially with its proud columns and stately windows, but it came without the crowds. In fact, I seemed to be the only person looking at the palace. I walked along the full length of it until I looked across the road and saw a nervous lion. The lion statue was in the park opposite the palace and looked terrified, reminding me of the lion in the *Wizard of Oz*. As I took a photo, I felt a raindrop land on my head, and then another, and another. Soon the sky turned into a waterfall, and so I sought shelter among the tall trees of the park. When it had subsided enough to allow me to escape, I decided to return to the hotel; after eleven days of constant movement, in seven different countries, I needed some rest.

On the way back, on a small area of wasteland, I noticed a small shelter made from boarded-up pieces of wood. Inside it were five merry men, all of them supping from cans of cheap lager. The whole group were laughing uproariously as one man sang a tuneless melody. His voice was loud and booming and his friends thought it hilarious. One of the men caught my eye. He nodded, tipped his can towards me in a jaunty manner and then smiled. I nodded back and waved. I could still hear the man's singing when I rounded the corner: vagabonds having fun.

8

Later that evening, I decided to finish my tour of Brussels in Grand Place, the place where I'd started earlier that morning. Tourists were swarming all over it, cameras in hand, starry wonder in their eyes. Children walked by, eating chocolate waffles as their parents swivelled their heads this way and that. In and among the crowds were some street performers: a violinist here, a juggler there and a few people dressed as statues. One performer was a dreadlocked man standing by himself. He was wearing headphones that were so loud that I could hear the unmistakeable voice of Bob Marley. He was dancing in front of a strategically placed cup, eyes closed with movements suggesting narcotic overload. His audience was only me. I watched him for a few seconds and then deposited a two-euro coin in his cup. I don't think he noticed. After one last, lingering look at Grand Place, I headed along one of the arterial streets towards my hotel. I had an early start the following morning. I had a train to catch to Luxembourg.

Top row: The magnificence of Grand Place; Tintin mural
Middle row: The Town Hall spire towering above the streets of
Brussels; Manneken Pis bottle opener; The actual Manneken Pis
statue
Bottom row: The Atomium; Scaredy-cat lion

Chapter 8. Luxembourg City, Luxembourg

Interesting fact: More people visit Luxembourg than actually live there.

My morning journey began at Brussels Central Station, a place full of dour-faced commuters and grey-suited train guards. Each guard sported a matching grey hat decorated with an orange band. Whenever two or more of them met, they kissed on the cheek, even the men: an appropriately continental thing to do.

The cavernous hall inside the train station was a place of frantic activity. One woman was rushing along, dragging a large suitcase behind her; somehow managing to avoid the people gawping at the large information screens. I went up to a self-service machine and pressed the button for English. A minute later, I had purchased a return ticket to Luxembourg City. With it clutched in my hand, I headed down some steps to a windswept platform, grabbing a take-away coffee on the way.

The platform was like all others in Europe – a waiting place for bored expressions and one-handed newspaper reading. Most of my fellow passengers seemed business-like, armed with briefcases and dark suits, but there were a few tourists too. I could tell they were tourists because, unlike the glazed faces of the regular travellers, their faces were full of concentration and eagerness as they studied the electronic information screens. I drained the last of my coffee and checked the weather on my phone. Luxembourg was forecast to be overcast and drizzly. Well, after the sunshine of Malta and Monaco, I could hardly complain. Ten minutes later, I looked at my watch and was delighted but unsurprised to see a double-decked train entering the station dead on time. When it stopped and the doors whooshed open, all the business people boarded, leaving the tourists in their wake. We hesitated, waiting for someone to make the first move; the last thing any of us wanted was to get on the wrong train. After a moment of nervous glancing, I finally made my move and climbed aboard. Everyone else followed. Luckily, it was the right train.

2

Three hours later, the train arrived in Luxembourg City. The weather *was* overcast and drizzly. Outside the station, I put my hat on and stared at Luxembourg. It didn't seem that inspiring, to tell the truth, because it looked like any other European city. The busy road in front of me was full of cars, taxis and modern buses. A large wagon transporting Magnum ice creams sped past sending a wave of spray as it did so. I decided to leave the central part of the city and head north to the old town, passing department stores, generic hotels and a McDonald's restaurant.

Luxembourg, sandwiched between Belgium, France and Germany, is one of the smallest nations on earth. A staggering 246 Luxembourgs can squeeze into the area of France. But compared to Monaco, it was huge – 1280 times bigger. As well as being one of the smallest nations on the planet, it is also one of the richest, with most of its cash coming from its banks. I passed a few financial institutions on my way, but ignored them until I came to a large bridge called Pont Adolphe, which overlooked a large area of forest and a railway line. The bridge marked the boundary between Bock, the old town, and the modern part in which I'd arrived.

I passed a gigantic Luxembourg flag rippling in the hearty breeze and then stopped at a golden statue of a woman holding a wreath. She was on top of a tall obelisk in the middle of a busy car park. A few empty coaches were nearby and a tourist train was waiting at the edge for passengers. It was already a third full with mainly Chinese tourists.

I looked up at Gelle Fra, the Golden Lady; even in the dismal conditions, she shimmered. First placed on her granite pedestal in 1923, she was a memorial to the thousands of Luxembourgers who had joined the Allies in World War I. Just then, a spot of rain landed in my eye and so I made my way towards a small shop just a few metres away.

The window display was full of plastic replicas of the golden statue. There were hundreds of them, ranging in size from just a few centimetres to ones so large that they must surely look ridiculous in any home. The shop also had shelves lined with white plates, all of them emblazoned with the face of the current Duke of Luxembourg and his wife. When I saw a gaggle of Chinese tourists heading my way, I decided it was time to leave.

3

The best church in Luxembourg City was Notre-Dame Cathedral, a double-spired building with a dramatically sloping roof. The road alongside the cathedral was called Boulevard Roosevelt, named after the former US president, which I walked along until I emerged onto a pretty little square surrounded by town houses. At one end, a trio of teenage boys were larking around, pushing each other, kicking water and generally making a racket. In the small square, their laughter and shouts were amplified by the stone buildings, which explained the policeman's sudden arrival. The teenagers stopped their antics and walked away sheepishly.

Avoiding the puddles, I walked towards the town hall. I found it at one end of another pretty square that doubled up as an outdoor market. Large cheeses, cuts of meat, pots of jam and bunches of colourful flowers filled most of the stalls, but the rain meant only a handful of Luxembourgers were browsing them. I stopped at a stall selling sausages and salamis. Long tubes were laid out on display or else were hanging down from a small bar along the ceiling. There was a man behind the counter with a thick moustache. He looked like a typecast sausage seller.

At first he spoke to me in German but switched to fluent English. "Are you wanting a particular kind of sausage?" he asked without a trace of humour.

I looked at a thick dangling sausage covered in some sort of white dust. "What's the white powder?"

"It is mould."

I was startled. "Mould?"

"Yes. It is safe to eat and gives the salami more flavour. It helps prevent it from spoiling. Would you like to try a sample?"

I declined, not because of the mould, but simply because I wasn't a fan of salami. I thanked the man and wandered around the other stalls until I spied a narrow archway. At the other side, I came to yet another square, this one called Place d'Armes, Luxembourg's main square.

Another set of teenagers were loitering around the edge of the square. This time they had skateboards and were keeping themselves busy by performing small-scale stunts, oblivious to the drizzle. I found an outdoor cafe with large parasols and ordered a four-euro coffee. My fellow patrons seemed well-to-do people, quite a high proportion of them looking like they were from the Far East. Luxembourg's banking sector attracted high flyers from all over the world, I knew, as was proven by the snippets of accents I caught: American, Russian, English and others that I didn't recognise.

The rain eased off slightly just as I finished my coffee. I paid the bill and walked onwards. Just beyond the square was a shopping street full of department stores. Did I need some shoes? No. Did I need a new jumper? No. What about an ornament for the living room? Yes! Actually, no. I headed in the opposite direction. The palace was nearby, and, if I timed it right, I might see the changing of the guards.

4

Luxembourg is the world's only Grand Duchy, meaning it is a nation ruled by a Grand Duke, as opposed to a King or a Prince, or even just a lowly duke. The 59-year-old Grand Duke of

Luxembourg was called Henri Albert Gabriel Felix Marie Guillaume, and bore more than a passing resemblance to David Bowie, I thought. He had once enjoyed lots of power in Luxembourg, but all that changed abruptly in 2008 when Henri refused to sign a law legalising euthanasia. After some head scratching and political to-ing and fro-ing, the politicians of Luxembourg passed the law anyway, thereby reducing the role of the Grand Duke to that of a puppet leader. Still, the Grand Duke does have some official affairs to conduct, and it is inside the Grand Ducal Palace that he conducts them.

The palace was along a narrow street guarded by a couple of brown-uniformed soldiers standing inside small booths. They had fetching red ties, jaunty black caps and some mean-looking machine guns. The palace was small but it did look grand, rising up over three stories, and was topped with a series of turrets and flags. During World War II, the Nazis had turned the palace into a concert hall and raucous tavern.

A horde of tourists arrived and stood with a guide. All were babbling excitedly, preparing their cameras for the changing of the guard. From stage left, a guard appeared – a young man with a definite paunch. With the tourists going crazy, I noticed a fourth guard marching from stage right. With a click of their heels and a swift manoeuvre of their guns, they replaced the guards in the booth, all the while ignoring the flashes and excited hum of chatter. After taking a quick snap, I left the guards and the Grand Ducal Palace and headed off to find some underground passageways called the Casemates.

5

Before 1867, Luxembourg City had been home to a strong fortress: so sturdy, in fact, that a French engineer described it as the best castle in the world, apart from one in Gibraltar. When Luxembourg became a neutral country in 1867, part of the deal was to demolish the fortress, or as much of it as possible. The only remaining parts are the tunnels and a bashed-in tower with weeds growing from its top reaches. Opposite the tower was the entrance to the Casemates. In their heyday, these tunnels were capable of holding 1200 soldiers and fifty cannons, and during World War II, 35,000 people managed to squeeze in them to escape the onslaught of dropping bombs.

"Bonjour!" said the man behind the glass screen.

"Bonjour!" I replied cheerfully.

The man then spoke to me in rapid French, but the only word I caught was *euro*. I nodded and handed over three euros, as dictated by the price board next to his window.

"Merci," he said.

"Merci," I replied as he handed me a ticket and small pamphlet. The man then spoke to me again but I didn't catch a word of it, but nodded as if I did, and then, to cement the illusion I could speak French, I said "Merci," again, followed by an authentically accented "Au revoir".

I entered the darkened catacombs and waited for my eyes to adjust. When they did, I saw that the pamphlet was useless to me. The man had clearly thought me a citizen of France or Belgium, because every word was in French. I couldn't be bothered returning to get a new one and carried on into the gloom.

6

The Casemates were eerily empty. As I made my way through one dark tunnel, being mindful to avoid the uneven and annoyingly low roof sections, I came across a sign written in French. It could have said: *Warning, unsafe passage ahead*, for all I knew, or *The best view is just ahead of here*, so I decided to carry on until I came to a curving stone staircase leading upwards. At the top, I found myself on a viewing platform of sorts. Gaps where cannons could be fired allowed light into the darkened recesses. After peering through one of the gaps, and not seeing much, I retraced my steps, clambering back down the staircase and traipsing along another darkened tunnel until I realised I was lost.

I trudged towards some light. Some more steps brought me out at another lookout point. I could see virtually the whole of Luxembourg City before me, and I wondered whether it might be prudent to yell for help. I looked at the leaflet again, but it offered no clue as to where I was or where I might have been. I headed back into the Casements again, feeling a little uncomfortable now, thinking about Minotaurs hiding in labyrinths. Damn my expertise at pretending to speak French, I thought. With an English-language pamphlet, things would be different. And where were all the other tourists? I lumbered back into the dark recess like a tin miner gone mad.

Eventually, I found an exit point and retreated from the tunnels with a dry mouth. Outside, a large group of tourists was about to enter, and I wondered if I looked like some sort of kidnap victim, just released from a dark hiding place. My eyes were like saucers and my head ached. To celebrate my newfound freedom, I found a bar and ordered a beer. I sipped it while financial workers of Luxembourg City wandered by with brollies and brief cases. Half an hour later, with a three-hour journey back to Brussels to look forward to, I decided to head back to the train station. Luxembourg City had been fun but it wasn't anywhere I'd be in a rush to get back to. As I crossed the invisible border with Belgium at high speed, I thought about the next city on my adventure. The following morning I was going to board another train and meet up with some friends in Amsterdam. The ninth nation of my whistle-stop tour beckoned over the horizon.

Top row: Luxembourg City's old town; The Golden Lady
Middle row: The spires of Notre-Dame; Changing of the guard
outside the Grand Ducal Palace
Bottom row: A more modern side of Luxembourg; A remnant of
the old fortress

Chapter 9. Amsterdam, the Netherlands

Interesting fact: Dutch people are the tallest on earth.

"Hello gentlemen," said the man standing beside a doorway depicting lurid pictures of naked couples. We briefly turned to face him but did not stop. We knew what he was going to say anyway because other men had already said the same thing.

He spoke louder this time. "Come on. I know you haven't come to Amsterdam for the flowers and clogs. You want smut and filth! Come in and see our show; we will give you what you want! All in a comfortable and safe environment! What do you say, eh?"

We didn't say anything. Instead, we carried on with our ramble around Amsterdam's famous red light district with the hundreds of other tourists doing exactly the same thing.

2

We were in Amsterdam to celebrate Jon's birthday. Jon was the friend who, in Veurne almost twenty years previously, had eaten a whole prawn because he hadn't known any better. My train ride from Brussels had been easy and stress free, taking me through Antwerp and The Hague before delivering me into Amsterdam Central Station after a two-and-a-half hour journey. The weather was pleasantly warm and, with an hour to kill before Phil, Michael and Jon arrived from the airport, I left my suitcase in the train station luggage store and went to find a coffee house.

Coffee houses are famous in Amsterdam. A green triangle in the window of one meant the cafe tolerated smoking cannabis within. The one I chose had the triangle. Inside, I took in the unmistakable and pungent aroma of marijuana. Across a few tables (in a sectioned-off smoking area), a few student-types were merrily smoking away. I walked up to the counter and ordered a coffee. Next to me, a man with long hair and loopy earrings was reading a menu – a grass menu. For ten euros, I noticed, he could buy two grams of Purple Power or 1.5 grams of Super Skunk. He could even purchase a pre-rolled joint for four euros. I took my tiny cup of coffee and sat down in the non-smoking section. Mr Longhair walked past me with a little plastic bag full of grass.

It was actually my fifth time in Amsterdam. The first time had been when I was ten, and I'd been with my parents. All I can remember about that visit was thinking how cold it was. My next three visits all happened when I was at university. Every year, around April time, a few of us would board a North Sea Ferry for high adventure in Amsterdam. On one trip, a friend of mine decided he wanted to visit a live sex show. When no one volunteered to go with him, he went by himself. An hour later, he returned looking ashen. Despite furious questioning, he refused to comment on what he'd seen, apart from one word – *sordid*. He never talked about it again. Ever.

My phone beeped. It was a text message from Phil saying they had landed at Schiphol and were about to board the train. I replied saying that I was waiting in a coffee house near the train station. Phil told me to prepare the joints. Fifteen minutes later, I took a last slurp of my coffee and went out to meet them.

3

After catching up and wishing Jon a happy birthday, we deposited our things in the hotel. Then the four of us decided to do something we had not done before: a canal boat tour. To get to a canal we had to walk through Damrak, one of the main thoroughfares of the city.

Damrak was mainly hotels, casinos, fast food restaurants, Amstel bars and tons of souvenir shops. As students, we had been especially taken with one fast food chain called Febo. Inside these small eateries, no one served anything; instead, the food was available to purchase behind small glass panels. For a few guilders, a hatch opened and out would pop a warm cheeseburger or some chicken nuggets and chips. Every meal for three whole days had been from a Febo. We were pleased to see the chain was still going strong. The only thing that seemed to have changed was they wanted euros and not guilders.

We arrived at a busy section of the canal and chose a boat that was leaving first. After taking our seats, the captain powered away from the jetty at a leisurely five knots. Ten minutes later, Phil, Jon and I were bored to death. The monotone voice of the person with the microphone, coupled with the gentle undulating motion of the barge, made our eyes feel heavy. Michael, as always, was enthralled.

"This is the gentleman's canal," intoned the voice, "and is one of three major canals in the city. It is named after some sixteenth century governors who..." My mind blanked out the rest of the sentence as I stared outside. A couple of grebes were swimming around near the edge of the canal. One dived down and, when it disappeared, I raised my eyes to absently stare at the buildings beyond, agreeing that they did look pretty enough. Suddenly my mind refocused onto the tinny voice. The man was saying something about cars going into the canal.

"On average, one goes into the water every day," he said. "And there are believed to be 30,000 bicycles at the bottom of Amsterdam's canals."

I looked towards the canal's edge, hoping to see a cyclist go in before my very eyes, but everyone seemed to be keeping well back. The number of cyclists was staggering though. Bicycles were everywhere, and all ages were riding them. Adults, pensioners, iPod-wearing teenagers – all of them cycling like there was no tomorrow. Specially made parking frames that contained the bikes when they were not in use were all along the canal paths. They looked like metal bushes. With the voice rattling off more information, we turned into another canal, and then another, until finally we arrived where we had started. We climbed out to find a Febo.

4

An hour later, we were wandering a busy street close to the red light district. The crowds were immense: most of them contained young men and stag parties, leery and full of beer. Some elderly couples shuffled about too, no doubt shocked at the profusion of sex shops and peep shows. Families steered small children away from the more obvious elements of seediness, and, in the midst of them all, cyclists tinkled their bells in an attempt to forge their own brief passageways.

Along one narrow street, we came across a series of shops selling sex paraphernalia for every perversion possible. Dildos, rubber hoods, whips, hoses and other less savoury items were on display behind large glass windows.

"My God!" uttered Jon, pointing to an enormous plastic penis. The thing was standing upright near a black leather gimp mask. Next to it was a full size mannequin dressed in what could only be described as clothing for a deviant. The dummy was shackled, wearing some bizarre black leather apparel that erupted into an oversized member. We were all mesmerized and horrified in equal measure.

We moved on, passing tall and elegant town houses filled with fancy filth. A young woman in front of us was handing out flyers, giving them to any group of men who passed. People took them automatically but when we approached, she decided not to give us any. A few steps later, Michael picked one up from the floor. It was for a clothes store. Clearly the girl had deemed us too unfashionable.

We came to another canal with an even greater concentration of people. It was called De Wallen, otherwise known as Amsterdam's red light district. We stood on a small bridge and surveyed the scene beyond. It looked like any other canal side street, but quite clearly it was not. A few strips of red neon signalled that sex was for sale.

~ 98 ~

"Well, we might as well get this over with," said Jon.

We nodded and crossed the narrow bridge to have a gander.

5

Amsterdam's red light district is a collection of streets and alleyways containing around 300 one-room cabins. Each cabin can be rented by a prostitute for her (and her clients') use. The area dates back to the Middle Ages, when Amsterdam became a bustling harbour and sailors in need of entertainment provided a steady flow of customers for the working girls. Fast forward a few hundred years and Napoleon's soldiers were the most common patrons of De Wallen, and the oldest profession in the world thrived. French troops visited the Dutch girls in such numbers that the authorities decided to bring in compulsory health checks for the women. This in turn sowed the seeds for the legalisation of prostitution in The Netherlands.

Large groups of men were leering at the girls in the windows, some stopping to gawk, but most hurrying past in a rather embarrassed way. We belonged to the latter group, not quite knowing where to look or place our hands. But there was also a sizable contingent of women wandering by. All were unashamedly pointing and staring, often giggling to themselves or making derogatory comments about the women behind the windows. The women were worse than the men.

"Hey, Frank," said a rotund American woman in front of us. She was in her sixties and had just spotted a girl in a window. Clearly they didn't realise they were in the red light district. "Is she a stripper?"

Frank looked but didn't say anything.

"Oh my God!" said the woman. "She's actually dancing in the window! And she's only wearing her underwear! The shame! Can you believe it, Frank?"

Frank, I was pretty certain, did believe it. He almost had his tongue out.

Perhaps because it was only mid-afternoon, the women along the canal side were mostly larger or older ladies, but all of them were quick with suggestive winks and smiles as soon as anyone glanced their way. At one window, a woman lifted her bra to show us what lurked beneath. She licked her lips as we scurried away to safety.

6

That evening, we decided to go out for a few beers to celebrate Jon's birthday. It was nice to be able to sit down and relax after two weeks on the go. One loud group of women in their early thirties paraded past us. They were dressed as naughty schoolgirls, with the bride-to-be wearing a veil and the obligatory L-sign. Five minutes later, a large group of young men blundered their way past our table. All Brits.

"What shall we do tomorrow?" asked Michael. "Because I was thinking of a museum."

Phil was first to scoff at this idea. "Oh, come on! A museum? We're in Amsterdam."

Michael ignored Phil and looked at Jon and me. "I was thinking of maybe the Rijksmuseum. It's full of paintings by Rembrandt."

"No," stated Phil. "I'm not going in a museum."

"Hang on," said Jon. "We're not youngsters anymore. I think we should do some culture for once. Every other time we've been here, all we've done is eat bloody Febos or swill beer. I agree with Michael, but I'm not sure about a Rembrandt museum."

"Okay," Michael said. "What about the Van Gogh museum?"

All eyes turned to me. Like Phil, they all knew I usually despised museums, especially ones full of paintings, but I knew Michael adored them. If we didn't visit at least one while we were in Amsterdam, then Michael would fly home disappointed.

Besides, Jon was right. It was about time we saw some culture rather than the usual medley of smut and bars. "I agree with Michael," I said.

7

The next morning, despite Phil's grumblings, we caught a tram to the Van Gogh Museum. All four of us paid the entrance fee and then quickly split up. Michael's modus operandi was to study each piece of art for a few minutes, then read the accompanying placard before returning his gaze back to the painting. Jon's method was slightly less time-consuming. He would study each picture and might read a few of the placards if he felt he needed something explained. Phil's method of looking around the museum was the same as mine – rush around everything at a constant walking speed, pausing only when someone in front of us blocked our way.

The paintings led us through a complete history of the great man's work, starting with paintings that looked nothing like what I'd expected. His early work was clearly of the traditional type, showing realistic scenes. Before long, though, Phil and I arrived at the painting he became famous for: *Sunflowers*. Both of us stopped.

Masses of people, most of them wearing headphones attached to small commentary boxes, crowded the famous painting. We manoeuvred ourselves so we could see the yellow flowers in a yellow vase. It looked almost childish to me, and I could not for the life of me see why it had become so famous, especially after seeing some of Van Gogh's earlier and, in my opinion, far superior work. I turned around to ask Phil what he thought but he had already gone. I found him by the entrance yawning. We had taken just twenty minutes to rush around the thirtieth most visited museum on Earth. Twenty minutes to see two hundred paintings and four hundred drawings made by Van Gogh. That was thirty pictures every minute, or one every two seconds. And that included climbing the stairs. It had to be a record.

Phil and I retired to a nearby café and ordered some coffee. Forty minutes later, Jon arrived and told us he'd not seen Michael for a while. We tried texting Michael, but he didn't reply; he was notorious for not answering his texts. In the end, we ordered another coffee and a cake each, and then a soft drink before Michael finally joined us, one and a half hours later.

8

Later that evening, after a few beers in Leidseplein Square, we decided it was time to visit the red light district again. It was either that or remain in the bar. The route we chose took us along some of the less-visited parts of the district. The ladies standing in the crimson-lit booths were all massively overweight and yet had squeezed into the tiniest underwear possible. One of the women proved enticing enough for a seedy-looking man, who disappeared into her booth without any embarrassment whatsoever. She closed the curtain behind her.

"Shall we club together for Jon?" Phil asked, gesturing to another buxom woman. "Ten euros each should cover it, I reckon."

"No thanks," said Jon.

"Spoilsport."

We walked across the bridge and a man trying to get us into his peep show accosted us. Posters of naked men and women hung on the outside of his establishment. The four of us wandered on, unable to stop staring at the absolutely gorgeous girls pouting inside the red-neon-lined windows. All of them were absolute stunners at this prime time of the evening. A beautiful blonde girl wearing only skimpy underwear noticed our gaze and opened her door, rushing out towards us. "Hey, any of you guys wanna come in and have fun?" We hurried away, heading for another bridge until we arrived back at relative normality. After one last drink for the road, we returned to the hotel.

9

After breakfast the next morning, I bid farewell to Phil, Michael and Jon. They still had a couple of hours to go before their flight back to the UK, and were planning to visit the Anne Frank Museum, something Phil was happy to do. As for me, I had no time left. I said my goodbyes and left them to it, glad I'd managed to squeeze Amsterdam into my hectic itinerary, even it had been for just a couple of days. I was soon sitting aboard the train to Schiphol Airport. My flight to Scandinavia was due to depart in just a few hours' time.

Top row: Red light district of Amsterdam; Damrak – home to a Febo
Middle row: Sunflowers for sale; Locked-up bicycles overlooking a canal; you can buy clogs in Amsterdam
Bottom row: A monument to working girls; Amsterdam is full to bursting with old town houses like these

Chapter 10. Copenhagen, Denmark

Interesting fact: Denmark has the oldest state flag currently in use by an independent country.

Angela and I met up in Copenhagen's Kastrup Airport. Both our flights had arrived on time and we wasted little time in jumping aboard the train to the city centre. Twelve minutes later, we stepped out into a bright and sunny Danish afternoon.

Our first impression of Copenhagen was not great. Outside the central station, just opposite Tivoli Gardens, both Angela and I were dismayed at the amount of litter. It was everywhere: piled up against buildings; trapped at the road edge; stamped into the pavements – you name it, there was litter. This was not the Copenhagen we'd imagined.

"What was Amsterdam like?" Angela asked. We were standing at a busy intersection waiting to cross.

"It was good. It was nice having a bit of a laugh with my mates."

"Did you go to the Red Light District?"

"Of course."

Angela gave me a look.

I said, "Everyone who visits Amsterdam goes there. It's a tourist attraction."

"Did you see any prostitutes?"

I smirked. "What do you think we saw? We even hired one for Jon."

"You didn't!"

I laughed. "No. He refused."

We arrived at the hotel. After unpacking, we went to see Tivoli Gardens, the world-famous amusement park and pleasure garden, the second oldest amusement park in the world. At a cost of 90 Danish Kronor (about £10), we thought the entrance fee a little on the steep side, but paid it nonetheless. Not knowing what to expect, Angela and I entered.

2

Tivoli Gardens first opened its doors in 1843 and offered a range of attractions that had wowed the residents of Copenhagen. The king at the time, Christian VIII, had commissioned the park so that the people of Denmark would have somewhere to amuse themselves and therefore not meddle with his politics. The gardens were noted for their sophistication and elegance, a place where visitors could wander around colourful flower gardens, experience noisy bandstands, brave state-of-the-art merry-go-rounds and even ride on scenic railways. When it got dark, lamps shone and sometimes fireworks exploded. The people of Denmark couldn't believe how lucky they were.

The buildings inside the gardens were also a major attraction. People imagined themselves to be in the Orient or North Africa due to the Chinese-style pagodas and the Moorish-themed Nimb Restaurant, a huge white building with a gigantic pastel green dome. With all this elegance and exoticness, Tivoli Gardens quickly established itself as one of the premier amusement parks of Europe.

Angela and I regarded the scene before us. The first thing that struck us was the number of children. They were everywhere, running giddily around, grasping ice creams or carrying large bundles of pink candyfloss like trophies. High in the sky was something called the Star Flyer, a tall tower that was swinging its occupants around a lofty carousel. Closer to ground level, but no less terrifying, was a rollercoaster called the Daemonen. Screams and yelps of delight came from it.

Despite the merriment going on all around, I felt disappointed. I'd expected tranquil lakes, areas of greenery, with perhaps an old merry-go-round spinning around. I did not expect the tacky amusement arcade in front of us. On a stage, a couple of entertainers pranced about, whipping up the largely juvenile crowd into rapturous hoots of laughter. Everyone under the age of fourteen loved it, but, for us, Tivoli Gardens was a bit too gaudy and too excessively touristy. It reminded us of Blackpool Pleasure Beach. After only thirty minutes, we decided to leave.

We left by the northern entrance, passing through Rahuspladsen, a large square dominated by the massive City Hall. Street entertainers were juggling, breathing fire or playing pan pipes under its shadow. Around the corner was a large statue of Hans Christian Andersen; the famous Danish author looked stately as he stared along the street.

Leading away from the square was Strøget, a long shopping street lined with familiar brands. Less familiar was the word *Slutspurt* written in many of the windows. Only later did we find out that this was Danish for *final push* or *sales*. Further along, sitting outside some dirty windows, were three vagabonds, two of whom were clearly intoxicated. The third man was asleep, a large wet stain along his trousers. A collection of plastic bottles lay littered around them. Everyone ignored them and so did we.

3

Nyhavn means New Harbour and is perhaps the most photographed place in Copenhagen. Outdoor bars, cafes and restaurants, with each of the colourful seventeenth and eighteenth century townhouses painted in reds, yellows, blues and oranges, lined it. The buildings overlooked a wide canal.

Angela and I wanted to go for a drink in one of the bars, but the crowds put us off. Every table was taken, packed with jostling and nudging people. Instead, we found a quiet spot next to a giant anchor and sat down with a bottle of water. "What's your impression of Copenhagen so far?" I asked as I took a swig.

Angela looked around. "It's nice, but not as nice as I expected. I think I was hoping for it to be...I don't know...maybe a bit classier." As if on cue, a man wearing a football shirt passed us and spat into the water. Angela shook her head. "Need I say more?"

4

The next morning, we followed a coastal pathway leading to the Little Mermaid. Angela had read that a lot of people ended up disappointed by the size of the sculpture, expecting it to be much larger than it was, but, as we approached, we felt the opposite reaction – it looked life-sized. A crowd of people were standing on the bank gazing at it while stallholders tried to hawk tacky plastic models of the statue.

The mermaid is linked to a famous story by Hans Christian Andersen, in which a young girl trades her mermaid tail for legs so she can marry a handsome prince. The story was written in 1836, but, almost seventy years later, it became the focus for an opera. And during one particular performance, a man named Carl Jacobson happened to be sitting in the audience. Jacobson was the son of the founder of Carlsberg Lager, and therefore an extremely wealthy man; as he watched the show, growing ever more enchanted with the tale, he came up with an idea. When the show was over, he commissioned a statue of the Little Mermaid, and the metal lady was unveiled to the public in 1913, just before the outbreak of World War I.

It survived the war, but was not so lucky in 1964. In that year, an unknown person (or persons) crept down to the harbour armed with a sturdy hacksaw. When Copenhagen woke the next morning, it was shocked to discover that someone had decapitated the Little Mermaid. It was akin to someone lobbing off the top of Big Ben or scratching the eyes of the Mona Lisa; the city was in uproar. The head was never found, and so artisans had to make a new one.

Twenty years later, someone sawed her right arm off, but two men returned it soon after. Welders managed to reattach it. Then, on a cold January night in 1998, the Little Mermaid's head was hacked off again. Across town, a figure wearing a dark hood made a grim delivery to a television station. It was the bronze head. The hooded figure disappeared without trace, but a feminist organisation claimed responsibility for the attack, saying they had removed the mermaid's head to highlight men's fixation with women's bodies. When Copenhagen's chief architect found out that the head had been returned, his reaction was almost ecstatic. "That's great," he told reporters. "To replace the head would have cost $14,000." The head was reattached; the Little Mermaid looked as good as new.

But the vandalism of the Little Mermaid was not over. Five years later, again in the dead of night, an explosion was heard in the vicinity of the statue. When police investigated, they found the mermaid's base curiously empty. After a quick search of the harbour, they found the bronze girl floating in the water with chunks missing from her wrist and knee. Again, craftsmen patched the mermaid up and returned her to the pedestal. No wonder the city's authorities have said they might move the statue further out into the harbour.

5

That night, after groaning at the extortionate price for a beer and a small glass of wine, Angela and I went to a supermarket and bought a bottle of decently priced red wine and some cheap plastic cups, and then found a bench to sit on.

As we sipped our wine, we watched people as they strolled past. A family of obese tourists waddled past, taking photos of everything and anything. Tall locals meandered around them like blond-haired sentinels. Across from us, sitting around the base of a fountain, were a group of Goth-looking teenagers. Some of them were smoking nervously, as if worried their parents might catch them at any moment.

Angela prodded me. A drunken man was weaving his way in our direction, bottle of wine outstretched, a bleary expression on his face. In his late forties, the man was grinning.

"Hello!" he boomed jovially in accented and slurred English. "How do you do? Might I sit next to you? I think you are English, yes? Every tourist in Copenhagen these days is English! Or Chinese!" Before we could say anything, he took the space next to Angela, enjoyed a large swig from his bottle and then placed it on the ground by his feet. He stared at it for a moment.

Angela and I didn't know what to do. The man suddenly looked up, as if he'd just thought of something important. "What wine are you drinking?" he asked, his words even more slurred. "I drink only fine Italian!" He guffawed and burped. Angela looked at me and mouthed, *"Let's go somewhere else."*

"Italian wine is better than Spanish or German, or that stuff they make in Australia." The man focussed on me. "I've been drinking all day and am very drunk. You must excuse my behaviour! But let me tell you one thing," he said, now staring at Angela's chest. "Your blouse is pretty! It looks so good! I like it!"

Angela shifted an inch towards me, but she was actually smiling. Even though our new friend was sloshed, he didn't seem the least bit threatening, and he certainly wasn't a vagabond. For one thing, his clothes, although a little dishevelled, were in good condition. His hair was a bit of a mess but he was cleanly shaved. It was then that I had a disturbing notion. Perhaps the man had noticed our bottle of wine and had assumed we were fellow drunkards in need of company. The man's eyes left my wife's chest and he reached down for his bottle. As he took another hearty swig, I asked him if he was from Copenhagen.

The man's gaze shifted up to me. It took some doing before he found focus. "Yes! I live in Copenhagen! But I am German. My mother lives here, and...well, I do too."

"Do you work here?" asked Angela, crossing her arms.

The man nodded. "Unfortunately, yes." He didn't elaborate and instead burped again, this time loud enough to attract the attention of a passing woman. She shook her head and hurried on. To her, we were three drunkards sitting on a city bench. Angela finished her cup and I drained mine too. I made an excuse that we had to go and meet some friends.

"So soon? Well enjoy the rest of your stay in Copenhagen," he bellowed good-heartedly. "And remember, a fine Italian wine is the best company on a summer's evening!"

6

For our final morning in Denmark, we headed back to City Hall. We arrived in time to join a group of other tourists for a guided tour. We looked at paintings and sculptures in an exhibit hall before ascending three hundred steps to the top of the tower. The view looked out over the whole of Copenhagen, right up to the coast. I could see the pan pipers below us, like tiny ants, setting up their amplifiers for the day's performance.

I walked over to one side of the platform to take a photo. A few minutes later, Angela joined me and hit my arm. "That's for wandering off by yourself," she said. "One minute you were there, and the next you were gone. I thought the man next to me was you. I embarrassed myself when I spoke to him."

I grinned. "Why? What did you say?"

"I said: If I wanted to kill myself, I wouldn't want to jump off here!" When he didn't answer, I looked and realised it wasn't you; I was mortified. He was just looking at me as if I was some sort of idiot. And do you know what he said to me?"

I shook my head.

"He said: 'I'm sorry, I do not speak English.'"

I laughed and then so did Angela.

An hour later, we were back at the hotel packing for our next destination: Stockholm.

Top row: Nyhavn – one of the most photographed places in Copenhagen; A windmill in Copenhagen
Middle row: The Little Mermaid – not so little; Copenhagen's City Hall
Bottom row: Inside Tivoli Gardens; Hans Christian Andersen statue; Danish guards near the royal residence

Chapter 11. Stockholm, Sweden

Interesting fact: In 2006, Sweden was the most generous nation on earth in giving aid to poorer nations.

The train from Copenhagen left dead on time. After leaving the central station at 6.30 pm, we crossed the long Oresund suspension bridge until we reached Sweden on the other side. It took fifteen minutes to cross from one Scandinavian country to another, where a yellow cross on a blue background replaced a white cross on a red background. Soon after, we stopped briefly in the town of Malmo to drop off a few passengers before the driver hit full throttle to fly across Swedish countryside at a considerable – but reassuringly gentle – speed. The countryside soon gave way to a landscape of conifers and the occasional lake, and, every now and again, things would go black as we travelled through tunnels. We made further stops at places I'd never heard of: Hässleholm, Nässjö and the intriguingly sounding Norköping. As advertised, the journey took a smidgeon over five hours. We walked to the hotel and went to sleep.

2

The next morning, the wind assaulted us the moment we stepped outside the hotel lobby. It was unseasonably cold in Stockholm for August, and I was glad Angela had brought my thick coat with her from England. As it was, my wife's hair was flying around her head in crazy circles. "Bloody hell!" she shouted above the melee. "I'm glad we didn't come in winter."

We headed for a bridge, keeping well back from the water's edge. It looked cold enough to freeze a body. Water surrounded Stockholm, with thirty percent of the city's area made up of canals, rivers and lakes. We crossed the bridge and came to Stockholm's City Hall. With its tall red brick tower, it reminded me a little of Oslo's.

"I know three interesting facts about this building," I told Angela. "Do you want to hear them?"

"It depends how interesting they are."

"Number one: It took eight million red bricks to build it, and if each brick were laid end to end, they would cover the distance from the UK to Italy."

"Quite interesting," admitted my wife.

"Two: Inside is something called the Blue Hall. It's where banquets are held after Nobel Prizes have been handed out."

"I thought you told me Nobel Prizes were given out in Oslo?"

I nodded, impressed that she had remembered. "But Norway only gives out the Peace Prize. Sweden gets all the others: Medicine, Physics, Literature and a few more."

Angela took this in. We were standing beneath the huge building. The tower was so enormous that we had to crane our necks to see the top where the Three Crowns, the golden emblem of Sweden, sat like a giant weather vane.

Angela said, "So what's the third interesting fact?"

"In July 2006, a man climbed to the top of that tower and jumped off."

Angela's gaze recreated the trajectory of the fall. She looked at the ground where he might have fallen. "Did he die?"

"Yes."

"At least it would've been quick."

We didn't really want to go inside the building – after all, we had done a city hall tour the previous day – but we did want to have a wander around its exterior. In a central courtyard around the other side, we came across a life-sized wooden horse, painted in blue, yellow and red. Its eyes had been painted in the style of an Egyptian pharaoh. It looked almost childish in its design and Angela took a photo of me pretending to feed it.

"These horses are famous in Sweden," said a voice. A man in his sixties, sporting a thick, bushy moustache, had approached from behind. If he'd had a helmet on his head and some animal hides strewn over his shoulder, he could've passed as a Nordic chieftain. He was a museum guide; when we told him we were just about to leave, he nodded and proceeded to tell us about the horse anyway.

"They are called Dala Horses. You see them all over Sweden. You can buy small ones in shops as souvenirs. They originally came from a part of Sweden called Dalarna, hence the name. People started making them about 200 years ago."

I nodded thoughtfully, wondering whether we would have to pay for the lecture. But Angela seemed interested so I didn't say anything.

"They became so sought after," continued the man, "that some families made a living from producing and selling them. They passed their skills down from generation to generation. Anyway, you said you were leaving, so please don't let me keep you."

There was an awkward moment when I felt I ought to pay the man but, in the end, I didn't have to because he simply walked away. We did too, heading into Gamla Stan, the old town.

3

Stockholm's old town consists of endless medieval cobbled alleyways, towering church spires and some of the grandest buildings in Stockholm. The founder of the city, a man called Birger Jarls, constructed a fortress there in the thirteenth century. One of the spires belongs to Storkyrkan, the Great Church, and Angela and I stepped inside it to see the largest medieval monument in Scandinavia. *Saint George and the Dragon* had been exquisitely carved from wood, with sections of it coated in gold.

"Okay, it is quite big," I admitted as we stared at the thing. George had been frozen in time as he slayed a nasty looking dragon. The winged beast was also being trampled beneath Saint George's steed's feet. According to the guidebook, the sculpture contained the actual relics of the great saint, though where they were contained we couldn't tell.

Back outside, we turned a corner and immediately recognised the square in front of us. The tall, thin buildings at the far end featured heavily on postcards sold in every tourist shop in Stockholm. It wasn't difficult to work out why – they looked almost fairytale-like with their pointed roofs, brightly coloured facades and chocolate box windows. The square was called Stortorget, and, on a cold night in November 1520, people living in the colourful houses witnessed a most terrible event, an event that became known as the Stockholm Bloodbath.

4

The Stockholm Bloodbath came about after the Danish King, Christian II, conquered Sweden. After being sworn in, Christian held a celebratory banquet lasting three days, and then, to show he meant well, he invited lots of prominent Swedish clergymen and nobles to the royal palace to have a private chat. They came willingly, because Christian had earlier granted them amnesty in return for their quick surrender. What they didn't know was that they were all on a secret list. At the top of the list was a heading: *Heretics and Enemies of the State.*

The evening of 8th November 1520 was cold, with ice on the ground. As night fell across Stockholm, more ice froze and people hurried to their homes to escape the chill. In the flickering hallways of the palace, in a scene straight from a *Hammer House of Horror* film, guards carrying lanterns and burning torches walked along; they tore into the great hall, marching the Swedish guests away to dank cells where they were accused of their crimes. Every one of them admitted to being a heretic, which was not that surprising, because they had all been heavily tortured. Regardless of how their confessions came about, the next morning, they were all sentenced to death.

Just before noon that day, a German mercenary called Jorgen Holmuth was waiting in the centre of the Stortorget Square with an array of axes, swords and heavy-duty knives. He was an accomplished executioner, and, as he rigged up a few scaffolds with nooses, people started appearing in the square, all of them citizens of Stockholm, forced to attend by the new king's soldiers. Whatever was going to happen, they knew it was going to be bad.

At noon, there was movement from the side of the square. Guards brought out a bedraggled figure, quivering in terror, with his hands tied behind his back. The crowd stirred when they realised who it was – one of their own bishops: a man of the cloth! The guards dragged the poor man into the centre of the square, the bishop crying and begging for mercy all the while. Holmuth the German calmly picked up a sharpened axe and lopped his head off in one swift movement. It rolled across the frozen cobbles, blood streaming for a few seconds.

The guards dragged another bishop out to meet the same fate. Then the German decapitated two more. The ground beneath Holmuth's chopping block was red with puddles and streams, but the killings were even not close to finishing. Next, fourteen Swedish noblemen were up for beheading, and, because of their status in society, Holmuth put his axe down and used a cleaner-cutting broadsword to dispatch them. Then it was back to the axe for the town's mayors, magistrates and councillors, followed by some prominent merchants. The heads were placed in barrels and the bodies piled next to them. And still it carried on.

At one point, a man in the crowd started weeping at the horror of it all. Guards dragged him to the centre, where Holmuth silenced the man by chopping his head off. Another man, this one a city barber, was dragged from his shop and executed for the simple reason of being in the wrong place at the wrong time.

The executions continued all day and into the night, heads and bodies piling up with gruesome efficiency. And, as Holmuth the German swung his axe with relentless regularity, other less speedy executions were taking place around him, with commoners being drowned or hanged under the scaffolds. By the time the madness ended, eighty-two people lay dead, and Holmuth went off to wash his hands and clean his weapons.

But the ghastly goings on were not over for the people of Stockholm. As the crowds watched, a platoon of guards carried all the heads up onto a nearby hill. Another group of soldiers dragged the bodies up too, and then the whole grisly pile was set on fire. The Danish ruler, King Christian, earned himself a new name after that: Christian the Tyrant.

5

Taking centre stage in Gamla Stan is the massive Royal Palace, a huge rectangular brick and sandstone building. It is the official residence of the Swedish Royal Family, protected by blue-uniformed Royal Guards wearing golden helmets with spikes on top. As we stood watching them, a film crew turned up. They quickly positioned their cameras while a platoon of guards assembled into lines. When someone gave the order, the guards stomped about with impressive gusto, swinging their weapons this way and that, and we wondered what the filming was for. Suddenly, the director yelled something and the marching stopped. The crew repositioned their cameras and the guards regrouped elsewhere. We waited for a bit, but then grew bored and walked away.

"Do you want to see the smallest statue in Stockholm?" I asked as we crossed another bridge spanning a side canal.

"A statue of what?" asked Angela.

"A boy."

"A boy doing what?"

"I don't know."

"Well you've sold it to me with that description."

We found the iron boy sitting on a small iron table in a courtyard behind the quite unremarkable Finnish Church. The boy was only a few inches high, and around his tiny table lay a small collection of coins, to which Angela added.

"Which place do you prefer?" I asked. "Stockholm or Copenhagen?"

Angela answered straight away. "There's no contest. Stockholm just seems more cultured than Copenhagen, and prettier too. Plus there's hardly any litter."

A group of camera-toting tourists arrived and began cooing over the small statue. We left them to it, deciding to search out a rather special street in Gamla Stan called Mårten Trotzigs Gränd, the narrowest street in Stockholm and named after a sixteenth century merchant who had once owned a few properties down the alley.

Composed of thirty-six steps, and only about 3ft wide, it did look remarkably narrow and I posed on one of the steps, my arms bending as they touched the sides of the alley. In the sixteenth century, Mårten Trotzigs' shops had peddled iron and copper, allowing him to become one of the richest men in Stockholm. It was fortuitous for Trotzigs that his rise to prominence occurred seventy years after the Stockholm Bloodbath, otherwise he might have been one of the victims. As it happened, though, he still met a grisly end when assailants murdered him on a business trip to the north of Stockholm.

6

After a hefty hike that left me breathless and Angela weary of my moaning, we arrived in Södermalm, an elevated district of central Stockholm, the once slum section of the capital. It is now the bohemian part of the city, home of the privileged and artistic. We stopped in Häckejäll (Hell's Forecourt) so I could catch my breath.

In the seventeenth century, local people believed that witches congregated in Häckejäll, kidnapping children to take them to the devil. This belief led to extensive witch hunts, culminating in the witchcraft trials of 1675. In them, many innocent people, including children, were killed as witches. One infamous story regarded a woman called Malin Matsdotter.

Malin Matsdotter was of Finnish descent; she lived in Stockholm for most of her life working as a part-time midwife. When her adult daughters accused her of kidnapping her own grandchildren (an accusation Malin strenuously denied – pointing out that she had no need to kidnap them because she could see them whenever she liked), she was tried before a court and accused of sorcery. She pleaded not guilty, of course, and so was sent away for torture. Afterwards, she still refused to accept her guilt, which, in the eyes of the courts, was the surest sign yet that she was a witch – after all, who but a witch could withstand painful torment without breaking?

At the time, Sweden was in the middle of a witch-killing frenzy. In the town of Torsåker, central Sweden, one single day saw sixty-five women and six men executed for being witches. All of them were beheaded and then burned. This was the usual method of dealing with witches, but *only* if they pleaded guilty, which they usually did – which was why Malin Matsdotter's absolute refusal to admit to being one was causing a bit of a problem. In the end, the courts decided that she would be burned *alive* at the stake. As a concession, they would tie a bag of gunpowder around her neck as a way of accelerating things.

On the day of her execution, guards brought the 63 year old to Hotorget Square, now a lively city-centre thoroughfare and home to the Royal Concert Hall, to meet her fate. Calmly, she took the necklace of gunpowder and climbed onto the pyre, protesting her innocence all the while. With a sizeable crowd watching, the pyre was set alight and, slowly and horribly, the flames reached Malin's legs and thighs. As fire danced around her, causing no end of agony, she still refused to admit she was a witch, even though doing so would have ended her suffering because a man with an axe was waiting nearby. She died a horrible death, but then something unusual happened. As the charred corpse was being removed, people started to question the testimony given by the witnesses, most of whom had been children. The evidence from one boy in particular, a 12 year old called Johan Johansson Griis, gave them the most cause for concern.

Johan Johansson Griis's infamous antics began at a young age. When his father died, he decided to accuse his own mother of being a witch. With the mass hysteria about witches in full swing, officials arrested, tortured and then executed the poor woman. This left Johan an orphan, but, instead of being full of remorse, he began to take great glee in fabricating tales of how his mother had abducted him and served him up to Satan. Each retelling became more fanciful than the last, and soon, sizeable crowds, a lot of them adults, began to listen to him. Over time, he established himself as something of an expert in witch behaviour, and then he upped the ante further by telling his now large audiences that he had learned to recognise witches. On one memorable occasion, Johan flung himself around the crowd before flopping to the ground dramatically. When he came to, he told his audience that a witch had been present, though he couldn't see exactly who. People lapped up the boy's tales and his celebrity status in Stockholm grew to such an extent that other children started to invent tales of witches kidnapping them. Instead of berating these wayward children for inventing far-fetched tales, people believed everything, and when these same children pointed at random women and accused them of being witches, the women were arrested. Scores of innocent women were executed based upon their ridiculous recounts.

Johan's downfall came when interrogators questioned him about his testimony involving Malin Matsdotter. Each time, the boy's story changed, and not just in small details, but in major events. He clearly had not seen her abduct children, and had made the whole thing up. When it was put to him that he had coached other children to be witnesses in the Malin trial, giving them stories to offer as evidence, Johan suddenly claimed that he himself was a witch. Unsure what to do, the authorities arrested him, put him on trial and sentenced him to death. Guards led Johan to the noose aged just thirteen, but his death ended the witch trials in Sweden. People no longer had the stomach for executing women who were almost certainly not witches, and those women who were awaiting execution were set free. Priests up and down the country were ordered to tell their flocks that all Swedish witches had been banished from the country and it was safe to go about their business.

7

"Look at her," said Angela, pointing to our left. We were still in Södermalm, near a large church, the place where locals had once prayed against non-existent witches. I looked and saw a gaunt, thin woman aged about thirty standing on one leg. She was standing opposite the church, barefoot and wearing only thin clothes; her mouth was flopped open. Slowly, she moved to her other foot and spread her arms for balance. She looked like a witch. The woman seemed oblivious of our interest, because, as we watched, she stood on tiptoe and shuffled backwards a few paces, her arms still outstretched. Then she shrieked like a banshee and shuffled towards Häckejäll with her straggly hair blowing about her head in the hearty breeze.

Just around the corner was the Butcher's House. It was a long pink building with lots of shutters. Angela asked me what was famous about it.

"A couple of hundred years ago, a disturbed man used to kidnap young women," I told her, "and take them back to this house. And then he'd kill them with his array of butchering instruments.

Apparently he was a qualified sausage maker. Some of the woman's innards ended up in his scrumptious pork products."

Angela regarded me solemnly. "You're making this up, aren't you?"

I nodded, smiling. The real truth behind the name was rather more mundane. Towards the end of the eighteenth century, generations of butchers had worked there.

"Oh," said Angela. "I actually prefer your version. Much more interesting."

We found a café and ordered some lunch. "How about we go to that Ice Bar next?" Angela asked.

The Ice Bar was back in downtown Stockholm, and was the world's first permanent bar made from ice. I cut into my salmon roll. "Can you handle vodka at two in the afternoon?"

"Can you?"

"I think so."

"I think so, too."

We finished our lunch, paid the bill and left the witches of Södermalm to get on with their antics.

8

Before we entered the Ice Bar, we had to don some impressive, space age silver Eskimo suits that came with mittens attached to string. Like arctic spacemen, Angela and I opened a doorway and entered the main room. As the room was kept at a constant minus five degrees Celsius, we could feel the cold immediately.

A long bar (made of ice, of course) lined one edge of the room, and opposite it were ice seats covered in what looked like animal hides. Everywhere we looked was ice and more ice. Even the walls were made from ice.

"What would you like to drink?" asked the barman, a young man wearing a Russian-style fur hat. We perused the menu, choosing one of the Absolut Vodka cocktails on offer. While he made our drinks, Angela asked him how long his shift lasted inside the ice bar.

"We work for three hours and then we can warm up again," he laughed.

"Three hours?" she said. "That seems a long time."

"Yes, but we are wrapped up warm and we are not always out here in the actual bar. It's not so bad."

A few minutes later, we were sipping our sub-zero drinks in glasses made of ice. Angela grinned. "This is the highlight of Stockholm for me. This bar is great!"

Forty five minutes later (the maximum time allowed), we were sitting in a cafe warming up. My feet had become cold inside the Ice Bar, but Angela had been right: visiting the ice bar had been a definite highlight.

For the remainder of the evening, we hit a few bars and had a meal in a Mongolian barbeque bar before retiring for the night. The next morning, after breakfast, we would be catching the ultra-quick Arlanda Express train to the airport to check in for our flight to Rome. We had finished with Scandinavia for the time being, and now Southern Europe beckoned once more. A quick fire tour of Rome, followed by an even speedier romp around the Vatican, would take my country count to thirteen. Over half way.

Top row: Dala Horse near City Hall; It's easy to see why Stockholm is called the Venice of the North
Middle row: The smallest statue in Stockholm; City Hall; Enjoying a vodka in the Ice Bar
Bottom row: Stortorget Square – scene of the Swedish Bloodbath; Storkyrkan, the Great Church; Gorgeous street in Gamla Stan

Chapter 12. Rome, Italy

Interesting fact: Italy has more masterpieces than any other country in the world.

I had my first and only altercation with an Italian stall keeper near the Spanish Steps. While Angela was busy inside a shop, I was merrily minding my own business taking a photo of a nice little side street. That's when I heard the commotion behind me. It took only a second to realise I was the focus of the commotion, because a middle-aged Italian man wearing a white apron was yelling at me. He was also flapping his arms and generally making it known I had somehow pissed him off.

"You move outta da way!" he shouted. "You mova away from my stall!"

I had to concede I was quite near his fruit and vegetable stall, but I couldn't fathom why it was making him so angry. Perhaps it was the heat: Rome was sweltering in 37° Celsius temperatures. I told the man to calm down and stop being such an angry brute. This didn't help. He flapped his arms some more and rushed up to me.

"You knocka my scales offa with your stupido bag!" he yelped, angrily jabbing his finger at my backpack. "Knocka it off with that!"

I looked at his scales and saw them sitting safe and sound on their perch at the end of a table. My bag was nowhere near them. I turned to face my Italian tormentor. "Look," I said. "Stop shouting and get a grip. I was only taking a photograph, for God's sake!"

The man looked like he was about to punch me in the head, or else smash my face in with his scales. He started yelling in Italian; with an audience of appreciative tourists, I smiled, shook my head and turned around, disappearing into the crowds near the steps. You cannot beat an irate exchange with a hot-headed Italian in the heat of August, I thought.

According to our guide book, visiting Rome in August was a bad idea. For a start, many of the smaller businesses and restaurants would be closed, their owners off on holiday somewhere, and then there was the heat. Italy's capital was notorious for becoming a sticky tinderbox in the searing summer sun. But after the wind and grey of Stockholm, Angela and I were looking forward to a bit of sun.

We were standing in the middle of a lovely bridge as the sun blazed down on our heads. Already I could feel the back of my neck and arms burning. In front of us was the Castel Sant'Angela, a circular fortress built by Emperor Hadrian as his mausoleum that ended up as a fortress for various Popes. It was large and bastion-like, and in most cities would've been a prime tourist sight, but here in Rome it was merely a sideshow to the A-list attractions.

We walked on, arriving at the back of a mass of people gathered in front of the Pantheon, the best preserved Roman building in the city. Its front was made up of eight gigantic columns that supported a massive pediment which lead to its enormous dome – the largest dome in the whole of Europe, no less. It seemed hard to believe that the Pantheon was two thousand years old.

The reason it had survived the passage of time so well was due to Papal influence. Almost five hundred years after its construction, the Pantheon was handed over to the then current Pope, Boniface IV, who turned it into a church. If he hadn't done so, it probably would have suffered the same fate as most other Roman buildings – abandonment, decay and then destruction.

Angela and I entered the huge building. Inside was a large collection of statues, as well as the tomb of the artist, Raphael. The inscription on his mausoleum said his bones and ashes were contained within. Above us, the large dome echoed with the constant hum of conversation. I turned to Angela and tried to stifle a yawn. It wasn't through boredom, it was due to fatigue. Even though it was only three pm, I suddenly felt weary to my bones.

"Let's go back to the hotel," suggested Angela. "You can have a nap and I can have a swim in the pool. You look like you need the rest."

3

The next day we were sitting on a subway train to see a pyramid. My long period of rest in the hotel had recharged my batteries somewhat, and, though my legs still ached from all the walking I'd been doing over the last three weeks, I felt much better for it.

Neither of us had been aware that Rome had a pyramid – but it most certainly did because, twenty minutes later, we were staring right at it. It wasn't quite up there with the Great Pyramids of Giza, but it did look striking. The Pyramid of Cestius was covered in marble and pointed 37 metres into the blue sky.

According to our guidebook, it was over two thousand years old and a magistrate called Cestius had built it. While in Cairo, the magistrate had seen the real Great Pyramids and was so taken with them that, upon his return to Rome, he decided to have his own commissioned. When he died, his family put him inside the pyramid with some of his possessions, but everything had long since disappeared.

The dulcet tones of a saxophone began as our second train journey of the day set off. A man in his thirties was playing it; with him was a small boy wearing a cap. As the train gathered speed, rushing through the dark world beneath Rome, the man whispered something to the boy, who then started dancing and moving slowly along the length of the carriage. It was a strange salsa, involving twisting arms and swirling hips, and one that bore almost no correlation to the music. Even so, all eyes were upon the boy, but then, a minute later, when he stopped, removed his hat and wandered the carriage cap in hand, people looked away. The only person who gave him anything was a little girl sitting opposite us who deposited a few coins in the hat after hounding her mother for them.

A few stops later, the train slowed down and stopped. The metro stop read: Colosseo. With scores of other passengers, Angela and I alighted and shuffled our way towards the exit. The man with the saxophone remained in the carriage with the boy, I noticed. We headed for daylight and to one of the Seven Wonders of the World.

4

Built by slaves and prisoners in 80 AD, the sight before us was one of pure Rome. If Paris had the Eiffel Tower, Sydney had the Opera House and London had Big Ben, then Rome's pride and joy was surely the Colosseum.

Tourists swarmed the thing. Armed with cameras, they hurried, scurried, pointed and gawped, or, like us, shielded themselves from the worst of the August heat. A couple of men dressed as Roman soldiers waited by one of the entrances, posing for photographs in exchange for some euros.

Fairly recently, a Roman soldier had made the news. Andrea Terlizzi was jailed for eight months for attacking an American tourist. Terlizzi told the courts that the American man had been wearing a Hawaiian shirt and had a cigar in his mouth, and so Terlizzi had assumed he would get a sizeable tip in return for a photo.

The American saw things differently. After handing over an undisclosed amount of US dollars for the photo, the Italian's reaction surprised him.

'In Italy we blow our noses with dollars' was Terlizzi's reported comment. He then called the American 'a son of a bitch, a Mafioso and a cuckold'. Things escalated when Terlizzi kicked the tourist to the ground. In the resulting drop, the American broke a finger. He got up and sought out the nearest policeman he could find.

Today's Roman soldiers seemed better behaved than the hothead Terlizzi, but the amount of money changing hands just to have photos taken with them seemed utterly ridiculous. We saw one woman hand over a twenty euro note. And this was for a photograph (that she took herself with her own camera) of the soldier pretending to hold a sword to her husband's throat. Even so, there was a queue of people waiting for their turn with the centurion.

"I'll tell you what," I said to Angela, "I'm going to buy a Roman soldier's outfit from a fancy dress shop and do this myself. I'll make a killing. This guy must be making...what...100 euros an hour? Even if he only averages forty or fifty euros an hour, and works an eight-hour shift, he'd still make...what...? 400 euros a day! Not bad for posing in a skirt and fluffy hat."

"I wish I could go back in time and visit Rome in the sixties," said Angela. We were waiting near the Arch of Constantine so I could get a photo of Angela in front of it. A trio of annoying cyclists were prancing around the arch, delaying us. The young men were taking stupid photos of one another, mindless of the people waiting.

"Back then," continued Angela, 'it would have been so romantic, so carefree and...so...free of tourists. People riding around on Vespas, people stopping for coffees beside a fountain, people having snacks in pretty piazzas – but now Rome is just one massive tourist overload. And this heat is too much. Can't we go? Take a photo somewhere else."

I looked at the cyclists. One of them was holding his bike in the air while his pal knelt underneath, pretending it was about to fall on his head. The third man was laughing so hard that he looked like he was about to collapse. I tried to work out what was so funny but failed to do so. If the bike had fallen, then that would have been funny. Or if a man dressed as a Roman centurion kicked one of them, then that would be hilarious. I stood for a moment, wishing for it to happen; when it didn't, and the trio of fools continued with their poses, I finally admitted defeat and we moved on.

5

We negotiated our way through the crowds, following a main road that led to a large white building. Men trying to flog paper umbrellas, stalls selling overpriced drinks and people pushing pushchairs littered our way, but we eventually arrived at Trevi Fountain.

To be honest, I had no idea what the Trevi Fountain would look like. I'd heard of it, of course, but had never seen a picture of it. And why would I? I had no particular interest in fountains, famous or otherwise. In my mind I'd imagined it to be a rather grand fountain with maybe a nice pool of water underneath. It would be something to take a photo of and tell people I'd seen it, but that would be about it. But I was totally wrong; Trevi Fountain was so much more than that. It was huge and beautiful. It was the best fountain in the world.

"When Audrey Hepburn was here in *Roman Holiday*," said Angela, "there were only a few people around this fountain." She gestured now at the multitudes in front, a sea of heads jostling for position near the mammoth waterfall that was as tall as the buildings surrounding it. Plumes of water were cascading downwards along its rocks and statues; a massive figure of Neptune stood in the middle. For me, I couldn't stop staring. It was only after being nudged and jostled for the fifth time that I decided enough was enough.

We moved with the crowds until we came to Piazza di Spagna. The square had once attracted posh tourists as part of their Grand Tour of Europe. The likes of Keats and Byron had probably once walked where we now trudged. In fact, Keats had died, aged only

26, in a building overlooking the square; it now houses a museum dedicated to him. But the crowds were not here for the old poets and writers; they were here for the Spanish Steps. It was to be our last stop in Rome.

6

"Will you stop yawning," said Angela. We were staring up at the 138 steps of the widest staircase in Europe. The steps had once linked a Spanish embassy at the bottom to the church at the top, hence the name.

"I can't help it. I'm knackered. I've been travelling too quickly. In fact, I think it's affecting my mental state. I had a weird dream last night. I'm surprised I didn't wake you."

"About what?" We moved out of the way of a large contingent of nuns. Most of them had cameras and guidebooks.

I shook my head. "It sounds bizarre, but a giant earwig – about three feet long..."

Angela shot me a look.

"... was in our house attacking the cats. They legged it out the catflap, leaving me with it. I was on the sofa and chucking pillows at it, but it just ripped them to shreds with its pincer things. It then started going for me and I was backed up against the wall. That's when I woke up. Who knows what would've happened if it had started biting me."

Angela smirked. "Why an earwig?"

"God only knows."

People everywhere were posing on the Spanish Steps, or gathering at the bottom taking photos. I couldn't believe someone had actually tried driving down them once. The incident in question happened on the morning of 13th June 2007. Somehow, a 24 year old man from Colombia, perhaps lost (and almost certainly over the limit) arrived at the top of the steps; instead of stopping and turning around, he decided to drive down. According to witnesses afterwards, people were literally diving out of the way, like something from a film. When the young man reached the first platform, he stopped the car and got out. After scratching his head, he then got back in and bumped his way down to the second platform. From there, he somehow secured the help of about seventy bewildered bystanders who between them managed to manhandle his car to the bottom. The Colombian was charged with drunk driving and damaging a historical monument.

"Shall we climb up?" asked Angela.

I shook my head. "I haven't got the energy."

"No, me neither."

We headed towards the metro station. After a meal in a pasta restaurant near the hotel, and a few drinks afterwards, we retired to our room to rest our weary heads. Our quick fire tour of Rome had drained me of all energy. I was glad that after visiting the Vatican the next day, we would be flying home for some well-needed rest and recuperation.

Top row: The Spanish Steps – just one of the magnificent
structures in Rome; Roman soldiers posing for photographs
Middle row: The Colosseum; Trevi Fountain
Bottom row: Rome's very own ancient pyramid; The Pantheon

Chapter 13. Vatican City, Vatican

Interesting fact: ATMs in the Vatican have a Latin language option.

The Vatican is the smallest country in the world. With a total area of just forty-four hectares, an astonishing 1245 Vaticans could fit inside the city limits of Leeds. Despite its minuscule size, the Vatican still packs a lot of punch. It issues its own stamps and has its own army – the ridiculously attired Swiss Guard. It also has its own newspaper (L'Osservatore Romano) and broadcasts from its very own radio station. Not bad for the most micro of all the microstates.

For Angela and me, the border crossing from Italy consisted of stepping over some white blocks of pavement at the edge of Saint Peter's Square (which we wouldn't have noticed had it not been for the guide book) and then we were in. It was one of the least interesting border crossings in all our travels, except perhaps for the one between Monaco and France. The first thing that struck us was the number of people. We thought Rome had been bad, but the Vatican was heaving.

2

Saint Peter's Basilica is the largest Catholic Church in the world, full of columns and archways, proud statues and Latin lettering – all of which paled into insignificance under the magnitude of its dome, the tallest dome in the world. Angela and I found a spot in the crowd to gaze at its beauty.

All around, people were staring in awe or pointing their cameras in the direction of the dome. Others gathered near the Colonnades, the columns that circled the Vatican's enormous square, with even more congregating outside the Apostolic Palace, the place where the Pope sometimes gives his Sunday blessings. We fought our way towards the centre of the square so we could look at a tall obelisk. We couldn't see much of it, but we did know that Caligula had plundered it on a visit to Alexandria in AD37. It supposedly had once held the ashes of Julius Caesar.

A large digital readout behind us said it was possible to book tickets for an audience with the Pope at 10 am the following day, which was too late for us, as we would already be at the airport. We set off moving again and passed a couple of Swiss Guards posing for photographs – free ones this time. With their orange and blue stripy pantaloons, floppy shirts and silly shoes, they resembled court jesters.

Swiss Guards, I knew, had to be unmarried men between the age of 19 and 30 with a 'good moral ethical background'. Pity the same couldn't be said about some of the Vatican's priests. I recalled reading an article describing one ex-Swiss Guard's experience with one. The priest had invited the guard for a meal, and as he served the steak and spinach, the man of the cloth mentioned that there would be no cake afterwards, because he, the guard, was to be dessert. The guard fled.

Angela and I made our way to the northern entrance of the Vatican so we could hand over our pre-booked tickets. As we sidestepped the masses, I wondered what the Pope was doing. What did a man like the Pope do in his spare time, if he even had some? And what would he think of all the tourists swarming over his abode?

Around 25,000 people pass through the Vatican's holy gates every single day, which, in a country of fewer than 840 residents, means lots of queuing. And ironically, despite being the holiest of all nations, it has a soaring crime rate. Unscrupulous chancers and pickpockets operate in abundance within the Vatican.

"It's always nice to walk past people queuing up," I said to Angela, as we sauntered past the unfortunates. Touts tried to offer us tours of the Vatican Museums but we waved them away; we had the tickets already and we had no wish to pay their extortionate fees for the same thing. At the front of the queue we showed a woman our tickets, and then entered the abode of God.

3

"Jesus," I whispered. "Just look." There were at least a hundred billion people inside the great hall, by my reckoning. It reminded me of being in the Tokyo underground, except multiplied by a thousand. "God help us (and He surely would) if there's a fire and we need to get out quickly."

In front of us was an escalator. It was jam-packed with mainly Japanese and American tourists, the former polite and quiet, the latter noisy, brash and twice the size. At the top of the escalator was a large sign that offered us two options.

"What do you reckon?" I asked Angela. One arrow pointed to the long tour, the other pointed to the short tour. Of course, I didn't really need to ask because I knew the answer. A few moments later, we were heading off in the direction of the short tour, soon arriving at the first of the exhibits.

Mummies, sarcophagi, canopic jars and large statues were everywhere. They startled us because they seemed so out of place. We felt as if we were in the Egyptian Museum in Cairo and not the Vatican. Various Popes had amassed the artefacts, plundering most of them during Roman times. "So these are all stolen goods?" asked Angela.

I shook my head. "I don't think anyone from the Vatican actually stole any of this stuff, I think they just...acquired them somehow. They'd already been stolen hundreds of years previously. The Popes just put them in a collection."

"Bloody nun!" I said a few minutes later. "Did you see her?" I had just been barged out of the way by a woman of the cloth. Angela laughed and nodded. The nun was peering at a mummy inside the cabinet that I'd just been looking at. There hadn't been any apology or anything, just a sharp shove. But it didn't surprise me that much; I'd had prior involvement with nuns. They had run the secondary school I'd attended in the 1980s. One incident from that time will stay with me for as long as I live. It involved a classmate called Dominic.

4

Dominic was never part of my circle of friends, but he was always there, in his wheelchair, rolling about, minding his own business. I would chat to him on occasions about this and that, as did plenty of others, but, for the most part, thirteen-year-old Dominic seemed to like his own company.

A year earlier, the powers that be at school decided to build a ramp to enable Dominic easy access to different floors of the school, saving him the unnecessary burden of having to negotiate his way up and down a series of horrible steps. It was a nice thing to do, and most schools in the UK were doing a similar thing at the time.

One day, for reasons unknown, Dominic decided to do something unbelievably foolish. After gathering a small crowd (me included), he told us that he was going to ignore the ramp and instead charge down the steps in his wheelchair. For him, we supposed, it was like being a stuntman, and, for the rest of us assembled at the bottom, it was a good chance to see him perform a dangerous deed with perhaps the possibility of him falling over as he did so. It was an exciting combination. After checking that no teachers were in sight, Dominic careered along at top speed, racing towards his imminent and bumpy descent. Everyone watched with glee.

Behind us, a dour figure dressed in blue had appeared, though none of us knew that then. It was Sister Jeffries, the school headmistress. Dominic, utterly unaware of the horror that was to follow, reached the top step and let himself go. While we all watched mesmerised, he jolted and crashed downwards, each bone-shaking step more hellishly fun than the last. Somehow he reached the bottom without toppling over, and the relief on his face was palatable. Amid the raucous applause, we suddenly became aware of a shrill shrieking. With fury etched upon her face, Sister Jeffries charged through the spectators until she arrived at Dominic. As we scattered for cover, I turned in time to see the savage nun whip Dominic across the face with her cane, and then again and again. An everlasting memory will be of the poor thirteen-year-old wheelchair-bound boy attempting to cover his already surgery-scarred face from the onslaught of a crazy nun.

5

Angela and I ambled away from the Egyptian collection, passing room after room of paintings, carvings, statues, bowls, jewellery, beautiful ceilings and much more. "And this is the short tour," I quipped as we stopped beside a Papal gift shop. Postcards, commemorative coins, Saint Benedict parchment, rosary beads and clay busts of the Pope could all be purchased. We didn't fancy anything and so moved on, bypassing the artefacts at top speed.

After pausing briefly to stare upwards at a golden ceiling (which was extraordinarily beautiful), we arrived in a large room full of animal statues. One striking piece was cast from white marble and depicted two vicious dogs attacking an antelope; one of the dogs had its teeth embedded into the poor beast's side. Another disturbing sculpture showed an almighty battle between a man and a bull. The man was sitting on top of the animal, stabbing it in the neck with a long dagger. His dog was also attacking the bull, and a snake too was getting in on the action, slithering up the side of the flailing animal to sup its blood. As bad as all this was, there was something worse. On the ground beneath the bull was a large scorpion. Depending from which angle I looked (and I looked from most) the scorpion was either attacking the bull's testicles or, more probably, had its pincer things thrust up into the bull's penis.

Either way, I wondered why the artist had depicted it, and how he had even thought of it.

"Look," I said to Angela when I found her at the other side of the room, "the end is nigh." I pointed at a sign which told us that down some steps was the grand finale of the tour – the world famous Sistine Chapel. We followed the masses downwards.

6

We entered the darkened hall of the Sistine Chapel, the finest building of the Vatican, the place where new Popes were selected, no less. As well as tourists, the large rectangular chapel was full to bursting with frescos and paintings: they covered every inch of the walls and ceilings, with only the floor and small windows free of art.

"Shhhhhhhhh!" screeched a security guard at top volume, causing a moment of relative quiet to fall across the chapel. Within two seconds, the noise was back up again.

"SHHHHHHHHHHHH!" he bellowed to no avail. I looked at the guard and thought he resembled an overstressed teacher. What he needed were some nuns with sticks. They'd surely get the crowds to behave with a good beating.

"SHUUSHHHH! QUIET!!!!" he boomed. It had no effect.

Angela and I took refuge in a far section of the large chapel; we eventually found a seat on a bench with a good view. I had a quick scan around, and then secretly brought my camera out from my pocket. There were signs all over the chapel saying that photography was prohibited and so I had to careful. As Angela gazed upwards at the frescos, I took a sneaky snap.

"YOU!" barked an angry voice. A security guard was rushing towards me. "Why you take photo? Put camera inside your bag." He stopped a few inches from my face. "And then zip it up, stupido tourist."

I did so, feeling all nearby eyes upon me. The security guard shook his head and returned to his hidden vantage point. I looked at Angela. She was glaring. "Why did you try to take a photo?" she hissed. "How embarrassing. I nearly died. You're a bloody idiot."

I nodded. It had been a foolhardy thing to do, but I was still looking forward to seeing what the photo looked like. I tried to speak in my defence. "It's not like I had the flash on. I didn't cause any harm to the frescos."

"That's not the point. The signs say no photography is allowed. You ignored them because you think the rules don't apply to you."

I decided to shut up. I was already losing the argument. Instead, I stared up at the works of artists such as Michelangelo, Raphael, Botticelli and someone I'd never heard of called Bernini. I tried to summon up the feeling of awe that most people said they got when they entered the Sistine Chapel, but I couldn't. Yes, it looked great, and the paintings looked of exceptional quality, but they certainly didn't wow me at all. Maybe it was because of the security guard or maybe because I was a heathen. I suspected it was the latter.

7

To get to the exit of the Vatican Museums, we had to walk down a spiralling staircase full of nuns. I eyed them suspiciously, but none paid me any heed as we passed. Standing once again in Saint Peter's Square, we looked at the famous basilica, with its distinctive dome glaring in the sun of August. It was a pity we didn't have time to go inside.

As we crossed over the border and returned to Italy, I mentioned to Angela that we had been inside the Vatican for a shorter amount of time than any other country we'd visited.

"What do you mean?"

"We were inside the Vatican for about three hours. That's the shortest amount of time we've ever stayed in any one country."

"Oh, I see what you mean."

An hour later, we were in a taxi on the way to the airport for our flight back to Manchester. A couple of weeks at home, and then it would be time to begin the second segment of my trip around Western Europe, a journey that would see both Angela and me visiting London, Lisbon, Madrid, Bordeaux and Cork in rapid fire succession.

Top row: Saint Peter's – the largest Catholic Church in the world; The strangely-attired Swiss Guard
Middle row: Spiralling staircase – beware of nuns; My sneaky photo inside the Sistine Chapel
Bottom row: A beast attacking a beast; Vatican street sign

Part 2

United Kingdom, Portugal, Spain, France, Ireland

Chapter 14. London, United Kingdom

Interesting fact: Medieval London had streets called Pissing Alley, Shiteburn Lane and Gropecunt Lane.

It cost three pounds each to secure our tickets down from Halifax, West Yorkshire to St Pancras Station in London. Six pounds in total! And when the Megabus pulled up, we were pleasantly surprised because the vehicle was modern and blue, and, best of all, contained a cantankerous Yorkshire git.

When the old geezer climbed out of his bus and opened the large luggage compartment on the side, he sighed. When Angela and I began shuffling forward with the other waiting passengers, he suddenly turned around, flashing fire from his wrinkled eyes "Nobody move," he barked.

We all stopped. All six of us stared at the man. He glared back as if daring anyone to cross him. It was half past five in the morning and all we wanted to do was get on the bus.

"No one gets on board my bus until I've checked your tickets," he said. "And don't even think about putting any luggage in here until I've checked you off my list." He waved the list as if it was a life or death document. A young woman started dragging her suitcase towards the open luggage compartment, seemingly unconcerned about the threat.

"You!" the driver roared. She stopped in her tracks. "Did you not hear me? Put the case down, love. Wait 'til you've been checked!" She did exactly that.

Judging by his manner, the driver had cut his teeth working on buses full of feral secondary school children. Five minutes later, once the man had checked everyone on the list, he allowed us to store our luggage.

"Okay," said Mr Grumpy after he'd arranged them to his liking. "You can climb aboard now."

Once we sat down, we realised the Megabus driver was not finished with us. This time, he had a microphone and was not afraid to use it. "Everyone put your seatbelts on," he instructed. "No excuses. We're going on a motorway, for God's sake!" As everyone scrambled to put their belts on, he carried on, his accent thick with Yorkshire flavour.

"And I don't want to see any bags by your feet. They should be in the overhead compartments. In an emergency, you need a clear exit. The last thing you'd want is to trip over your bag. So, in two minutes I'm going to walk down the aisle and check."

A man across from us stood to put his bag in the overhead compartment. The driver waited until he had finished and then spoke into his microphone. "I don't want lots of chattering either. I need to concentrate. And don't ask me to put on the radio; it's not going to happen. And listen carefully to this: the toilet is for emergency use only. Emergencies only! So sit back, relax and enjoy this Megabus service to East Midlands Parkway. We'll be making a few stops along the way to pick up a few more passengers, but once we reach the Parkway, you'll be able to catch the train to London St Pancras and my job will be done." When we finally moved off a short while later, the coach was silent. Probably just as he liked it. Total megabastard, I thought.

3

We arrived in London five hours later. From St Pancras, we caught a black London taxi to the hotel. The taxi driver was a friendly chap in his late forties. We got chatting and I asked him about *The Knowledge*, the rigorous test that all London cabbies had to pass in order to gain their licences. In it, a cabbie is required to learn every street and landmark, past and present, so they can decide, within seconds, the best route from point A to point B.

"Yeah, it took me four years and three months," he told us, his cockney accent coming through the speaker system loud and clear. "It was the hardest thing I've ever done."

I whistled at the thought of how long it had taken the taxi driver. "Did you do it in your spare time?" I asked.

"No, not at first. For the first two years, I tried to learn it on weekends and evenings around my job. I used to be a bank manager, believe it or not. But I failed the test five times in a row, so I had to give my job up. We had to live on just my wife's wage, which was hard, you know, but worth it in the end."

When we eventually stopped outside the hotel, the meter reading was £26.30. "Let's just call it twenty-five, eh?" the taxi driver said. Who said that all taxi drivers are scoundrels?

4

After we'd checked in, Angela and I caught a tube towards Westminster so we could get some lunch. As we raced through the subterranean tunnels, I started reading a newspaper that someone had left on my seat. The lead story described a heroic event from the previous day. On a busy rush-hour platform, a woman had been about to board a train. For just a moment, she let go of her four year old son's hand (so she could get her baby and pram on board) and the boy slipped through the gap between the train and platform. With only a few seconds to go before the doors of the train closed, the woman did the only thing she could think of: she screamed the place down. As people stood 'frozen in shock', a man suddenly appeared. He threw himself to the platform floor, reached down and pulled the bewildered boy to safety. After calmly handing the child back to his mother, he disappeared back into the crowd. No one knew who the mystery man was.

Angela and I emerged from Westminster Tube Station, the sight of the Houses of Parliament and its even more famous clock tower, Big Ben, greeted us. It was actually the first time either of us had seen either structure up close, and they looked every inch the icons they were. On a nearby road, an open-topped bus trundled past, its upper deck full of eager tourists, all snapping off photo after photo despite the murky conditions of a British summer's day.

I wondered whether any MPs were inside the Houses of Parliament, working out ways to cover up their expenses, but as it was summer, they were probably on holiday. We moved across the road to a cafe overlooked by the London Eye and got involved in our own scandal over expenses. Two sandwiches and a couple of coffees came to over £30!

"Jesus!" I exclaimed when I saw the bill. "Eight pounds fifty for a ham sandwich! That's insane. Did you see how much ham was in there? About ten pence worth, I reckon, if that."

"It's not actually called Big Ben, you know," said Angela, ignoring me moaning about the prices. "Big Ben is the name of the bell inside the tower. Not many people know that."

"I don't care about Big bloody Ben. All I care about is that sandwich. I could've bought a whole ham for that."

Angela turned to face me. "Okay, you've made your point. Your sandwich was a rip off, and so was mine. But this is London. We knew it was going to be pricey. We've just got to accept it."

I nodded glumly, pulling out three ten pound notes from my wallet and placing them in the leather folder. I was buggered if I was going to leave a tip as well. I still couldn't get over the fact that each mouthful of sandwich had equated to two pounds fifty.

5

The last time I'd been in Trafalgar Square was in 1990 as a student. A whole bunch of us had hit the square to celebrate New Year's Eve, and, though I can't remember much from that night, I can remember looking at the statue of Nelson atop his huge column and thinking that it was bloody big. It still looked big today, as did the square itself. But the whole place was snarled up with red

London buses and black London cabs. Trafalgar Square was one big traffic jam.

Tourists were spilling out from the nearby Charing Cross tube station, adding more humanity to those already congregating around the fountains and stone lions. Families with children grasping ice-creams, foreign tourists clutching cameras and guidebooks, as well as the occasional policeman: all vied for position under Horatio Nelson's Statue. He appeared to be gazing out across London, a stoic expression on his face despite the antics beneath him.

"Covent Garden should be called *Convent* Garden," I said as we headed towards the popular tourist site. "It used to be the garden behind an abbey and convent."

Angela didn't comment.

"But for some reason it dropped the 'n' about five hundred years ago."

She remained mute.

"Do you want to hear any more interesting facts about Covent Garden or are you satisfied with the one you've heard already?"

"I'm satisfied with the one I've heard already."

In my ignorance, I thought Covent Garden would be a small park, perhaps with birds and squirrels huddled around a picturesque lake, but Covent Garden was a shopping centre, albeit one that specialised in small boutique-type stores. I was disappointed from the moment we arrived, but Angela's reaction was the opposite. After following her around a few stalls, I grew bored, and so Angela suggested I find a bar to get a drink, and she would meet me later. I thought it was a good plan and wandered off for a pint in the Lamb and Flag.

6

The Lamb and Flag had been Charles Dickens' favourite watering hole, and was, according to records, the oldest pub in the area.

Before it acquired the name Lamb and Flag, it was known as the Bucket of Blood, due to the bare knuckle boxing that used to go on behind its doors. I walked under its red awning into the darkened bar and ordered a pint of London Pride. I took it to an empty seat by the window.

Like other solo patrons of the bar, I fished my phone from my pocket and checked my emails. After that, I reconfirmed the flight times for the next few days. We were heading to Lisbon the day after next, and then, from there, flying on to Madrid. I wanted to check that everything was okay. It was, and so I put my phone away and took another sip of my beer. I had to make it last, though; I had thirty minutes to kill before meeting up with Angela again. With nothing much else to do, I retrieved my phone from my pocket and decided to play the time-wasting game extraordinaire: *Candy Crush*.

7

We made a lengthy walk to the Tower of London. Along the way, we lapped up a view of Saint Paul's Cathedral, wondering how on earth it had survived the Blitz without being damaged. For fifteen pounds we could have climbed to a viewing platform in the dome, but we quickly decided against it. "That's the problem with this city," I said to Angela. "They charge too much for everything. Fifteen quid to climb some steps. Twenty quid to go on the London Eye. Two hundred pounds to buy a sandwich. It's all one big rip-off."

The Tower of London was one of the few buildings in London to survive the Great Fire of 1666. It is also where the Crown Jewels are kept, guarded by the odd-looking Beefeaters guards. Of course, the Tower of London is probably most famous for the executions that were carried out there. During the reign of Henry VIII, two of his wives got their heads chopped off in the tower. But executions, off and on, carried on until 1941. The final execution was of a German paratrooper named Josef Jakobs.

Jakobs was an unlucky spy. On the day of his capture, he had parachuted from a plane over Ramsay, Huntingdonshire, breaking his ankle on the plane's fuselage on the way out. As he floated downwards over the English countryside, some keen-eyed members of the Home Guard looked up and spotted him. He was promptly arrested upon his landing. When police searched him, they found a radio, some forged papers, five hundred British pounds and, best of all, a large German sausage. During Jakobs' trial, he was convicted of spying and sentenced to death. He was executed by firing squad inside the Tower of London in 1941.

The entrance fee to the Tower was £19.50 and so we reluctantly walked past it, staring at the turrets and battlements instead. Besides, the queue had also put us off anyway, especially with a few drops of rain coming down.

All of a sudden, the heavens opened. Big fat dollops of rain came down, merging into a solid deluge of water. People giving away free newspapers became inundated with pedestrians wanting one as protection against the elements. We grabbed a couple too, trying in vain to cover our heads with the flimsy publications as the rain came down like an opened drain. In seconds, the roads became rivers, the pavements slick and slippery. People in open-topped buses were screaming, and so were we as we raced for the nearest tube stop. Eventually, sodden and shivering, we negotiated our way down the waterfall that masqueraded as steps until we reached sanctuary. According to the newspapers the next day, a month's rain had fallen over central London in just two hours.

8

The next morning, the rain had stopped, but London was still wet. We paid for some tickets to board a sight-seeing ferry plying the Thames, and, fifteen minutes later, we were receiving a running commentary from an amusing young man with a microphone. He told us he was an apprentice riverboat captain, a training period that would last between five and seven years. "Unless I drown first," he quipped, "because I can't swim."

We passed the Tate Modern, Cleopatra's Needle, St Paul's Cathedral, the Globe Theatre, numerous bridges and a shiny building made of an immense sea of blue glass, which the guide told us had been designed by an Italian architect who'd turned out to be an unemployed window cleaner. A few people tittered. "Before I talk about anything else," the man said, "I'd just like to inform you that was my best joke."

He did tell us some interesting things as well. For instance, none of us realised that the word *wharf* actually stood for 'warehouse at river front', and, as we approached the Tower of London, he started telling us about the Bloody Tower, the place where Sir Walter Raleigh had been imprisoned before his execution. "After his head was lopped off," said the guide, "it was embalmed and given to his wife. She kept it in a velvet bag for 29 years."

We all looked at the towers, and at Traitor's Gate (the Thames entrance to the Tower of London), trying to work out which one was the Bloody Tower. The young guide put us out of our misery. "A lot of people ask me where the Bloody Tower is, and I tell them all the same thing. We can't see it from here in the river because it's blocked by those bloody trees."

A short while later, the ferry stopped near Tower Bridge. Since the ferry was making a return journey from where we started, Angela and I alighted.

9

We wanted to visit the London Dungeons, another prime tourist site of London. When we rounded the corner near it, perhaps the most horrendous queue devised by man confronted us. It even beat anything in the Vatican. I sighed heavily.

"So what do you want to do instead?" asked Angela.

I shrugged. "Anything's better than this." I gestured to the queue. It hadn't moved a millimetre. "How about walking up the river to go on the London Eye?"

"Because you'll moan about how much it costs."

She was right. I would moan. But at least we would get a good view of London. We left the queue and headed back to the Thames.

Along the way, we passed the replica of the Golden Hind, which, like the original ship, had circumnavigated the globe back in 1980. Further along was the Clink Prison Museum, built on the site of a once notorious London prison. High on the wall outside it was a mock-up of a gibbet, a gallows-like structure where the decomposing bodies of criminals would once have been suspended to deter any other would-be criminals.

We walked along a lengthy promenade populated by street performers. Some were dressed in metallic-looking costumes; others were spinning plates in the most ingenious of ways. One man had attached super long arms to himself and tried to cuddle passersby, and one person was dressed up as Mickey Mouse, but ahead of us was our goal: the London Eye.

To bypass the queue and obtain a couple of express tickets cost us £60. But with the money we'd saved by not seeing anything else, I felt it almost justified. The views were impressive, though: we could see virtually the whole of central London. The only thing spoiling it was the weather. The dismal amount of light filtering through the clouds had cast the city in a dull mixture of browns and greys.

"London's not as high rise as I expected," said Angela as we neared the top of the ride. I nodded. I too had assumed the capital would be full of skyscrapers and towering office blocks, but, apart from the Shard and the Gherkin, there was hardly any. And as well as being relatively low rise, it was not a particularly pretty city. Yes, there were pockets of beauty, such as Big Ben and the Houses of Parliament, but it certainly didn't have the wow factor of, say, Prague, New York or even Tallinn, at least from above.

Back on terra firma, we decided our trip to London would not be complete without a visit to Buckingham Palace. We fought our way to the railings, looked at a few red-uniformed guards and then took a few photos. Seeing the guards reminded me of something I'd seen on the internet. Footage had shown one palace guard marching up and down while a young Colombian tourist walked alongside him, mimicking his movements. With his pal filming things, the man decided to have some fun. As well as walking alongside the marching guard, he also pulled faces and generally acted the fool. The guard in question marched on, his face giving nothing away, until, that is, he suddenly lost it and – quick as a flash – he shoved the annoying young man hard in the back. To me, the young man had deserved everything he got.

"Right," I said, "Big Ben, tick. Houses of Parliament, tick. Thames River cruise, tick. London Eye and Trafalgar Square, tick, tick, and now Buckingham Palace ticked off the list. What next?"

"Harrods," said Angela.

"Harrods?"

"Yes. Harrods."

10

Harrods is possibly the most famous department store in the world but to me it was no different from any other. It was full of items that I had no interest in buying. There were sections dedicated to jewellery, household goods, clothing, food and even vacuum cleaners. One section was full to the brim with Christmas trees, decorations and all sorts of festive paraphernalia, even though it was only August. The only discernible difference I could see between Harrods and any other upmarket department store, apart from the inflated prices, was the number of shop assistants. They were everywhere, all of them immaculately turned out and sickeningly servile.

The food section was interesting, though. Harrods was famous for its expensive caviar: in a display cabinet were tubs of the stuff. One small container of Prunier caviar was selling for £170. It would just about fill one sandwich.

But Harrods was not for the everyday shopper. It was for the super-rich, or tourists wanting to buy the cheapest thing possible so they could walk about town with a Harrods bag, which was exactly what we did. A box of Harrods breakfast teabags cost us £8.50, but came, as we knew it would, in a Harrods shopping bag. We left the store with our heads held high and our shopping bag swinging proudly. We found the nearest London Underground stop and headed back to the hotel. It was time to pack our bags for Lisbon.

Top row: Aboard the London Eye; Angela and Big Ben
Middle row: The Tower of London; Downing Street; Red-
uniformed guard
Bottom row: Buckingham Palace; Harrods

Chapter 15. Lisbon, Portugal

Interesting fact: Portugal produces more cork than any other country.

Standing in the centre of a sun-drenched Lisbon, Angela and I agreed it was a good-looking city: maybe not quite up there with the supermodels of Rome or Paris, but still a place to turn heads. The old town's understated beauty was full of red-roofed buildings and twisty cobblestone paths. A clutch of proud-looking statues and gorgeous old town houses littered wide boulevards, which were also home to lively bars and street cafes. And up on a hill, a medieval castle ruled supreme. All in all, Lisbon looked great.

2

Our journey began at Gatwick Airport; it was not a pleasant start. The young man with side-parted hair behind the check-in desk took our printed-off reference sheets and tapped something into his computer. Then he looked up and said, "I'm afraid you'll have to pay a twenty pound fee because you didn't send your passport details online. You'll have to go to that desk over there to pay, sir."

"I beg your pardon?" I asked, miffed. "Twenty pounds? How was I supposed to know you needed our passport details beforehand?"

"Because it states, quite clearly, sir, that you have to do this on the website. And it's twenty pounds each." It was a well-rehearsed line and one he had undoubtedly used many times before. He looked past me and gestured that the person behind should come forward.

The man was a robot: there was no point arguing the toss with him. I sighed, grabbed our sheets back and then dragged the suitcases to the other desk. Angela and I waited behind another couple who were busy paying their fine. The man was grumbling about low-cost airlines and that in the future he would only travel with proper airlines. I listened as he told the middle-aged woman behind the desk that the whole thing was a cleverly disguised racket to extract cash from unsuspecting passengers. She smiled and nodded but took their money anyway. The couple walked away. The man was fuming.

It was our turn. The bored-looking lady behind the counter asked for our printed sheets and passports. After typing something into her computer, she looked up. "Forty pounds, please."

I nodded, plucking my credit card from my wallet. There were four people behind us: the desk for paying fines was almost as lucrative as the London Eye. Before I handed my card over, I asked the woman what the money would be used for, especially since forty pounds was a fair bit of money: more than the cost of the flight itself, which I helpfully pointed out to her.

Her expression changed. "I'm sorry?"

"Well, whenever we've flown British Airways or Alitalia, for example, I haven't provided my passport details beforehand, so I'm just wondering what the money is going to be used for?"

The woman looked a bit confused. She saw the queue behind me and sighed. There were seven people now, and passengers like me were probably the bane of her life. "The forty pounds fee is because you didn't forward your passport details in advance."

I nodded. "I know that, but that wasn't what I asked, was it? I want to know what the money will be used for."

In my head, I tried to summon an image of an airline minion rushing around trying to locate the special ledger containing the special form. After discovering its whereabouts, he would dip his quill in squid ink, and, using italic handwriting, would record our passport numbers. Then he would send it off at top speed (by motorbike courier) to passport HQ where the Civil Aviation Authority would sign us off on a passenger manifest.

The woman said, "It's used to update the passport numbers."

"Okay. How so?"

"Well, I've got to fill a couple of boxes in."

I nodded knowingly. "Like all other airlines do for free. So what you're saying is: your airline charges forty quid so you can spend ten seconds filling a box in on a computer?"

The woman nodded. We handed over the money and walked away, disgusted and quite rightly a little bit angry. Despite this, Lisbon turned out to be a real treat.

3

The Elevator de Santa Justa is over a hundred years old and looked it. Designed by a pupil of the man who came up with the Eiffel Tower, it was up a busy side street and looked big, blocky and black. It was our first morning in the Portuguese capital and we were standing in the queue for the short ride upwards. A few minutes later, we reached the small viewing platform at the top. From there, we climbed a rickety spiral staircase to an even smaller viewing platform.

"Wow!" said Angela, as we stared down at the terracotta-roofed buildings. "Lisbon is lovely." We could see the Atlantic Ocean at the edge of the city, and tiny people below waiting for red and yellow trams. Behind us were the Carmo Ruins, remnants of a fourteenth century church that had been partially destroyed in a devastating earthquake in 1755. Behind the ruins, accessible via a walkway, was a quiet square littered with small trees and a small cafe. A couple of old gents were sitting enjoying espressos as they chewed the fat. A cat strolled out from an alleyway and lounged in a sun spot. It was an almost perfect Mediterranean setting.

From the square, Angela and I walked along a cobbled street lined with tram stops. Lisbon is famous for its trams, and photos of them were on virtually every postcard in town. We arrived at Praca do Comercio, a large seafront square, a focal point for taxis and sightseeing buses. In the middle was a statue of an old king sitting proudly on his horse. King Jose I was surrounded on three sides by fabulously grand buildings, the fourth side taken up by the ocean.

Prior to 1755, none of the present buildings existed. In that year, one of the world's most devastating earthquakes struck Lisbon.

4

At just before 9.40 am on the 1st November 1755, in an area of the Atlantic Ocean two hundred kilometres off the coast of Portugal, subsea tectonic activity was about to unleash a massive earthquake. For the people of Lisbon, the morning was a busy one, with folk moving around on foot or traversing the cobbles on horses and carts. Early morning markets would have been doing a roaring trade, as would the city's inns and metalwork shops. Craftsmen, pedlars, lords and peasants were all going about their daily business as normal.

Then everything changed. Lisbon started shuddering. Within seconds, the city's once sturdy buildings began to collapse to the ground as gaping fissures (some up to fifteen feet deep) tore into the ground. As heavy timber and stone tumbled, hundreds of people were crushed to death, while others fell screaming into yawning cracks. Amid the devastation, horses slipped into deep holes, dragging their carriages full of terrified passengers along with them. The once bustling streets of Lisbon were now in the grip of one of the most powerful earthquakes in history, a relentless assault that reportedly lasted for six minutes.

As the aftershocks came and went, thousands of people were already dead. While survivors rushed into any open space they could, well away from any buildings that might still collapse, they hoped that the worst was over. But they were wrong. In the square where the Royal Palace stood, a crowd of people were witness to a most startling event. The ocean in front of them was receding, moving so quickly from the shore that it left fish flapping on the dry surface. Old wrecks that hadn't been seen in years were now suddenly revealed, as were boxes of cargo that were thought lost forever.

While people considered this strange event, fires were breaking out all over the city, mainly sparked by toppled candles and ovens. The fires spread, soon turning into an inferno that consumed building after building. The brand new opera house was razed to the ground, as was a hospital, burning hundreds of patients to death. Lisbon had never experienced anything so cataclysmic, and then, approximately forty minutes after the last tremor shook the city, another hell was unleashed.

Seemingly from nowhere, a tidal wave rushed in and engulfed Lisbon. As it raced over the square, it destroyed the Royal Palace and washed untold treasures from the city's libraries and museums. People, who had been standing at the water's edge just moments before, were now being swept inland by the cauldron of an incoming tide. Anything not tied down was washed away, and the wave came at such speed that the only people who could outrace it were those on horseback. With an unimaginable mixture of earthquake, fire and now tidal damage, Lisbon was under siege, and it only ended when the water finally returned to the ocean. By the time the dust settled, eighty five percent of the city lay in ruin and between thirty and forty thousand people were dead.

It took a year to clear the destruction. The king ordered that the city should now have widened boulevards (to allow any future surge to channel away from residential quarters) and strong rectangular buildings (to withstand earthquake damage), but, even with these precautions in place, he developed a phobia about sleeping inside enclosed spaces. He ended up spending his nights in specially constructed royal tents and pavilions on the outskirts of the city.

5

The sea now looked pleasant and calm. Lisbonites were taking advantage of the sun by having picnics at the water's edge. On the opposite side of the inlet was a huge white statue of Jesus Christ, based upon the more famous one in Rio de Janeiro. Built in 1959, the *Sanctuary of Christ the King* stood, arms spread, overlooking a large red suspension bridge that resembled San Francisco's Golden Gate Bridge: a juxtaposition of world icons.

"You want marijuana?" said a whisper behind me. I turned to see a shifty-looking gent with keen eyes and dirty fingernails, though it was his gold necklace that caught my eye first.

I shook my head and he disappeared into the crowd. Angela wanted to know what he'd said; when I told her, she looked shocked. "He was trying to sell drugs? Here, in broad daylight?"

I nodded. "Why? Did you want some?"

We turned away from the ocean towards the centre of the city, passing under something called the Triumphal Arch: built to commemorate the 1755 earthquake, it was a huge grey edifice covered in statues, columns and emblems. Through the other side was Baixa, a large pedestrian area full of shops and cafes. We picked a table overlooking a collection of street entertainers, including a man dressed up as Mozart, and another kitted out like a soldier from the future; best of all, though, was a man in a hat who was hovering in thin air, balanced only from his thin walking stick.

As we ate, with the chatter and laughter of happy tourists passing us by (including two nuns armed with cameras and ice-cream waffles), I looked at Angela. "I like Lisbon. I like it a lot."

"Me too."

6

"You want hashish?" whispered a man who approached from my right. Our eyes met and I shook my head. He didn't look quite as devious as the earlier man, but his darting eyes were similar. He disappeared into the crowd looking for other potential buyers.

Angela laughed. "Again! You were asked again. What is it about you they see? No one's ever asked me if I wanted to buy drugs. Not even when I was a student. But that's twice someone's asked you. I reckon they see something shifty in you, something...criminal."

Further up the hill was our main goal of the afternoon: the Castle of Saint George. Traipsing up the incline ahead of us was a family of three: Mum, Dad and a little girl aged about six. Dad was taking a photo of his wife and daughter.

Like all good tourists, we patiently waited for them to finish, not wanting to risk our necks in the road busy with motorists and trams, but after the seventh or eighth pose I grew restless. When Dad passed the camera to mum so she could take some snaps, I decided enough was enough. Dragging Angela with me, we stepped into the road just as a tram hurdled past. It missed my heels by what seemed like inches. When we reached the safety of the pavement again, I looked back at the family. The three of them seemed blissfully unaware. The little girl was now sitting on her father's shoulders posing for another photograph.

"If I'd been killed," I said to Angela, "that girl would be able to look back at the photo, all nice and smiley, as the British man's head was being sliced off under the wheels of a tram in the background."

Angela laughed. "Stop being so melodramatic. The tram was miles away."

The sound of peacocks heralded our entrance into what was regarded as the place where Lisbon was founded. The castle was just as it should have been: turrets, cannons and rocky fortifications. It was the place where Vasco de Gama had held a reception with King Manual I after discovering a route to India. The view was great from the lookout points, and we spent a good while simply wandering around discovering it all.

7

The taxi journey to Belem Tower proved interesting because of our driver. She was a lady of advanced years who seemed to dislike pedestrians with a passion. After speeding off along the tram lines, veering like a maniac to avoid being sucked into the ruts, we came to a sudden, abrupt standstill. We were at a zebra crossing of sorts. The pedestrians waiting at the side of the road were evidently not locals because they were hesitating, tentatively putting their feet onto the crossing while nervously eyeing the traffic.

BEEP! blasted our driver. *BEEEEEEP!* she blasted again, causing the family to jolt into action. They rushed across at top speed, dragging their children behind them like luggage. Our taxi driver shook her head, muttered, and after another sharp beep to finish things off, we were off again.

Belem Tower looked extraordinary, an L-shaped battlement facing the sea. It was full of turrets, arrow holes, along with a section sticking out that had given it its distinctive shape. Built in 1520, it had originally been on its own island, but now was merely part of the coastline. Just next to it was a small cafe, where we decided to sit to have a refreshing afternoon drink.

"Lisbon's surprised me," Angela said, gazing out at the water. Yachts and small ferries were out there having a merry old time. People were ambling along the water's edge. "I can't believe we've not been here before. It's so unpretentious. I love it. In fact, I think it might be in my top ten places."

She picked up the guidebook. After leafing through it for a few minutes, she showed me a photo and passed it over. It was a fairytale-looking palace in place called Sintra, thirty kilometres northwest of Lisbon. It used to be the summer retreat for the Portuguese monarchy, according to the caption.

"We can catch a train there tomorrow, if you fancy it?" Angela said.

I looked at the photo again and then at a fuller description. As well as the palace, Sintra also had a castle, a small town centre and it looked like a nice day out. "What time does the train leave?"

"Every fifteen minutes."

The next morning, our train journey to Sintra took us through the outskirts of Lisbon, which were not as pretty as the city centre. Ugly, concrete apartment blocks and heavily graffiti laden walls lined the tracks. What was it with graffiti around railway embankments, I thought? It was the same everywhere: as soon as you left the train station, there it was. Soon enough, though, the concrete and painted scrawls made way for Portuguese countryside and, in no time at all, we found ourselves arriving into Sintra Station.

The weather was hot and the sky was an almost perfect blue. As we left the small train station, we took in the compact town of Sintra. It had a pretty central square surrounded by a fine set of red-roofed, grand-looking buildings, a lot of them cafes and gift shops. For some reason, it reminded me of *Trumpton*, a TV program I used to watch as a small child, which was about a carefree little town busy with townsfolk. Sintra looked just as untroubled and quaint, and I could understand why Lord Byron had once claimed that it was the most beautiful village in the world.

"For pity's sake," I said twenty minutes later. We had just rounded the third uphill curve towards the castle and, instead of offering the salvation of some flat terrain, it offered more of the same: another curving hill shrouded in forest.

Angela ignored me and so I huffed along behind her, thinking how my lungs and legs were suffering with the effort of it all. The last time I'd been so worn out had been in Liechtenstein. Around the next bend, a coach came trundling up past us, full of happy, and camera-wielding, tourists. Angela called them lazy but I called them clever bastards.

The Palace da Pena, when we eventually arrived, looked like it belonged in Disneyland. It was decked out in yellow, pink and white, with red turrets, stone battlements and large archways.

Tourists posed in defensive booths, leaned against stony walls or pointed at ugly gargoyles. The bus we had seen earlier was parked at one end, its occupants already gone. After a walk around the walls, we arrived back at the front and spotted a queue.

"Are they waiting to go in the palace, do you think?" Angela asked.

"Probably." I was already dismissing it, looking for somewhere to get a drink.

Angela nudged me. "Well, I want to go in. We've come all this way, and I think it'll be nice to see how the kings and queens of Portugal once lived."

"What? You really want to join that queue?'

Angela nodded. "Unless you've got anything better to do...?"

Ordering a few beers probably wasn't the correct response. And so began the worst museum visit ever.

9

It would not have been so bad had it not been for the eager beavers in front. They were blocking any rapid movement along the narrow passageway with their loitering. For what seemed like an eternity, we stood pressed against those in front, while the slowcoaches at the head of the group marvelled over teapots and plates. Eventually, we shuffled forward and briefly glanced at the pots and pans until we arrived at the back of the mass again.

"Satisfied?" I said to Angela as we moved an inch forward, this time to look at a bed a princess had once slept in. "We're queuing up to look at things we don't even want to see."

"Oh, stop moaning. That's all you seem to do nowadays: moan. Oh, it's too expensive; oh, it's too far away; oh, there's people blocking our path because they're enjoying themselves. Moan, moan, moan."

I grumbled to myself. The main culprits causing the delay were a couple in their late twenties, unaware of the logjam behind them.

Both stood blocking the narrow aisle again, reading some information signs and then looking at the boring things behind the ropes.

"GET OUT OF THE WAY!" I felt like bellowing, but of course did not dare. With a hefty security presence inside the museum (making sure cameras were safely stowed away), there was no way I could get away with such an outburst. So instead, we waited, and waited some more, with me muttering under my breath, until they moved on.

"You spoilt that for me," said Angela, half an hour later as we finally reached the exit. "You realise that, don't you?"

"I know. I'm sorry."

"Just try to be more positive next time we're in a museum."

I scoffed.

"Just try."

In the centre of Sintra, we found a relatively quiet café. The traffic was horrendous, backed up tail to bumper with coaches, cars and even a tourist train. I'd read somewhere that the road from Lisbon to Sintra was one of the most congested in Europe. Looking at it now, I could well believe it.

"I wonder why you hate museums so much," Angela suddenly said. "I've never known anyone as bad as you. I know I'm not a major fan, but you break out in a cold sweat at the thought of going in one."

I bowed my head in mock shame then looked up. "I can't help it. It's a personality disorder."

"No it's not. You're just a heathen. You admitted that after the Sistine Chapel."

With nothing more to say on the matter, we finished our drinks and walked around the town where I bought a small fridge magnet of Sintra. Afterwards, as we made our way back to the train station, I had to admit that it had been an enjoyable day out in Sintra. But we needed to get back to Lisbon to pack. Later that evening, it would be time to say goodbye to Portugal and head off to Spain, the sixteenth country of my supercharged trip around Western Europe.

Top row: Panorama of Lisbon; Angela outside the Belem Tower
Middle row: Elevator de Santa Justa; Sintra Palace
Bottom row: Lisbon's Triumphal Arch; A tram of Lisbon

Chapter 16. Madrid, Spain

Interesting fact: There is no tooth fairy in Spain. Instead, there is a tooth mouse.

Prior to arriving in Madrid, my only other flirtation with Spain had been a boozy visit to the Canary Islands. Like thousands of other young Brits in the mid-90s, Tenerife had seemed so exotic, so foreign, especially when I was armed with a wallet full of pesetas that could be exchanged for a jug load of cheap beer. Back then, riding on a banana boat before hitting the bars of Playas de las Americas had seemed the height of sophistication, the epitome of carefree fun. And if there was a pile of vomit on the floor the next morning (or afternoon), then I knew the night had been a success. But all that was in the past. Angela and I no longer needed to be cradled among our own kind while abroad. We did not crave the full English breakfast while reading an expensively imported British tabloid and nor did we need to see the Union Jack flying on a beach full of pot-bellied lobsters. No, now we craved culture, and therefore chose Madrid as our stop in Spain. Even better was the price to get there. For some unfathomable reason, Iberia only charged £30 to fly from Lisbon. For once, I was not moaning about the cost of things.

2

Even though Angela and I were veterans of the underground, managing to negotiate our way around cities such as Tokyo, New York, Rome and even the capital of Uzbekistan without mishap, the Madrid metro caught us out.

The first issue was getting through the turnstiles. There were three of them: Angela was going through one, I was in another; as I negotiated mine, I could see that Angela's suitcase handle had somehow got caught on one of the metal barrier spikes. While she battled with it, annoying the people behind her, I decided to carry on through mine so I could help from the other side. In my haste, I unfathomably left my own luggage behind, causing blockage number two. I couldn't go back – the metal arms offered a one-way direction only – and, with the press of people staring at my luggage and me as if I was some sort of idiot, I looked around for help. A man in a blue uniform was already on the case; after pressing some buttons, and then manhandling the turnstiles, he got both of us through, luggage included. Our problems were not over though, not by a long chalk.

As soon as the train set off, I knew we were going in the wrong direction. It was annoying because we'd followed the signs correctly. I sighed and looked at Angela. I could tell she was blaming me for the mistake. We got off at the next stop and, as commuters arced around us, we studied a map of the metro network. "I don't know how it happened. Plaza de Espana is there," I said, pointing at the map. "We got on the train here. And now we're over there. It's insane."

Irritably, we dragged our cases to another platform and waited. Then we got on another wrong train.

"Jesus," I said as we sped through the darkness. "How did it happen again? We followed the signs!"

Angela didn't say anything. Instead, she shook her head. All we wanted to do was to get to the hotel to drop off our bags, and now we were on the third train to nowhere.

When it stopped at the next station, we dragged our suitcases off the train again, lugged them over a bridge and crossed to the opposite platform. Then we stood waiting for a train to take us back to the original metro stop. It was déjà vu of the worst kind. Finally we got on the right train and arrived at our destination.

3

The next morning we set off to see what the Spanish capital had to offer. Quickly, we realised that it was full to the brim with large and beautiful buildings, all standing on wide and stately roads. Everywhere was an architectural sight to marvel at, some with horses and chariots on top, others with golden orbs, almost all with statues attached somewhere on their facades.

The streets were cosmopolitan, with a healthy mix of olive-skinned Spaniards, white-faced North Europeans and a large contingent from the Far East. Men in suits, teenagers in crop tops, students with iPods and tall black men selling fake handbags plied the busy streets of downtown Madrid. After a walk through Plaza Sol, a square packed to bursting with street performers, Angela decided to stop and look at some handbags.

The tall black man in charge of the impromptu stall surveyed the street with a practised eye. The Madrid police had a heavy presence, and if they caught him they would move him on and perhaps ask him some awkward questions. All over the city, men just like him were wandering around with large white bags slung over their shoulders, full to the brim with counterfeit goods. Whenever they found a suitable spot, they would lay the contents down for a quick-fire selling opportunity.

Angela pointed to a brown fake Prada bag. The man picked it up and handed it to her, keenly looking at everyone around him. His height helped with this; he was like a spindly meerkat. While Angela inspected the bag, the man explained how good it was, and how to adjust the strap, never once taking his eyes from the street.

"How much?" Angela asked.

"Thirty euro," the man whispered.

Angela shook her head and handed the bag back.

"Okay, how much you pay?"

Angela looked at me, wanting me to offer a price. I shrugged. "Twenty," I said.

"Twenty-five," the man countered, standing on tiptoe to see over the crowd of heads.

Angela nodded and handed him some notes. The man pocketed the cash, passed the bag over and scooped up his pile. We walked one way, he the other. The whole transaction had taken less than one minute.

4

Plaza Mayor is Madrid's most famous and grandest square. A line of splendid buildings surrounded all four edges, all of them the same height, and all of them featuring sweeping arches and balconies. From these elevated viewpoints, the gentry of Madrid would once have enjoyed the spectacle of bullfights, royal pageants and, before that, the executions held during the Spanish Inquisition.

With an inquisition in operation, an almost carnival atmosphere would have filled Plaza Mayor. Food stalls, ale vendors and temporary seating stands were all brought in, with seats facing the centre of the square. In the very middle was a pyre. It was where the condemned person was dragged, usually accused of heresy, and given a final chance to repent: if they did, they would be garrotted before being tied to the pyre; if they did not, they were burned alive. Either way, it was good entertainment for the crowd.

Angela and I sat down for a drink at one end of Plaza Mayor. Instead of platforms for inquisition trials, it was now home to statues and street performers. The most striking entertainer was a fat man dressed as Spiderman. His belly was flopped inside the blue and red Lycra suit. As we watched, a young woman approached him, and the pair conferred for a moment. The spandex superhero nodded and followed her to some nearby seats. After some waving and cajoling, the woman's boyfriend joined them. As she stood with the camera, Spiderman pretended to do battle with the man, freezing mid-punch, and then posing with him in a headlock. After collecting a few euros, the overweight Spiderman wandered back to his spot in the square.

A man selling sunglasses, a woman selling stringy trinkets and then a penniless beggar approached our table in quick succession.

We waved all of them away. Plaza Mayor was full of such characters. Across from us, a pretend bullfighter was flinging his cloth with gusto while a few tourists took some pictures. Spiderman was walking around, but looked bored, as was a woman dressed up like a headless ghost carrying her head under one arm.

"Here we go again," I said, spying the man with a scraggly beard and unkempt clothes coming towards us. "This is getting ridiculous." But instead of bothering us, or anyone else, he found an empty spot in the square and produced a tiny flute from his pocket. I soon recognised the tune – the main refrain from *Star Wars* – which was repeated over and over. People walked past him without a second glance, others avoided him completely, but still he played on. In the end, I felt sufficiently sorry for him that I went over and handed him a two euro coin. He thanked me and stuffed it into his dirty trouser pocket. Then he carried on with the one tune he knew.

5

That evening, Angela persuaded me to go for a tapas meal. I'd never been for one before and she thought I'd enjoy it. We found a quaint little restaurant just along from Plaza Mayor and perused the menu. When the waitress appeared, we ordered a trio of dishes: Spanish stew, tomato toast and an intriguing item called forest sausage. The first thing to arrive was a plate full of thinly sliced pork covered in oil.

"What's this?" I asked Angela as I stared at the greasy mess.

Angela grimaced. "I'm not sure." She knew I was not a fan of oily food. At home, I even had to dab bacon with kitchen roll before I could stomach it. "I think it must be the Spanish stew, because it's not the toast or sausage.

I tentatively picked up a slither of meat and watched as the oil leaked over both sides. My finger was slick and my mouth was slack. What sort of maniac would describe this abomination as stew? Stew had vegetables and potatoes, not just bits of fatty meat in greasy oil. I flopped it back down on the plate. It quickly became submerged under a layer of grease.

The next plate arrived. It was a ceramic bowl full of red oil. Swimming inside the bowl were a few slices of sausage. No wonder the restaurant was empty, except for the old man drinking at the bar.

"This isn't tapas," I announced, "it's...crapas."

Angela looked at the forest sausage. It had never seen a forest, unless 'forest' in Spanish translated to *vat of vegetable oil*.

The third plate arrived and was a piece of toast with the thinnest layer of tomato sauce gracing the surface. Oil had been drizzled over the orange coating, which made the toast glisten.

I regarded my first tapas meal solemnly and silently. Angela broke the silence. "We have to eat some of it. Pass me the napkins and I'll mop some of the oil up. If I dry the pork, you can put it in the bread." The bread was the only thing edible on the table, and I wondered where the nearest McDonald's was. In the end, I managed to eat some tiny fragments of pork, and even a few bits of sausage, but only after I'd used four napkins to dry them out. When the waitress came with our bill and asked whether everything had been okay, like millions of other Brits, we nodded and said it had been fine. We left the restaurant still ravenous. Ten minutes later, we were gorging inside an all-you-can-eat buffet restaurant around the corner.

6

The next day, we had a few hours to spare before our flight to France, and so we visited the huge and long, white Royal Palace, a building full of columns, grand rectangular windows and crowds of people. It was bigger than expected, larger than Buckingham Palace, but we had arrived too late to see the changing of the guards. Instead, Angela and I stood looking through the railings.

"This might be the best royal palace I've seen so far on my trip around Western Europe," I said.

"Really? How many have you seen?"

"Buckingham Palace," I said, counting it off on my fingers, "then Oslo, Liechtenstein, Monaco, Brussels and Luxembourg. Plus Sweden and Denmark, and now this. How many is that?"

"Nine."

"But yeah, this is probably the best."

We left the Royal Palace and ambled through pretty squares and even prettier buildings until we came to a museum dedicated to ham. Intrigued, we found ourselves in a high-ceilinged shop selling hundreds of hams. They were dangling from the rafters, lined up on shelves or being sold from a counter. Along one side of the shop, a long side bar offered small sections of cut ham with bread. It wasn't a museum; it was a busy eatery. It even served beer and had a slot machine. "Now this is my kind of museum," I said to Angela. "One that serves beer and sells ham sandwiches! Well done to the curator."

Back outside, we ambled past the oldest restaurant in the world. According to our guide book, the Botin Restaurant had first opened its wooden doors in 1725, and painter Francisco de Goya had once worked there as a waiter.

"It can't be true, though," said Angela, "can it?" The restaurant appeared closed but there was a man standing outside wearing shades, a security guard by the look of him. "I mean, there must have been restaurants before 1725. Didn't the Romans have them?"

I nodded. "Probably. But this *is* the oldest one, at least according to the Guinness Book of Records. Why don't you go over and ask him?" The security guard crossed his arms and looked over at us.

"Why don't you?"

"Because I'm not that bothered." I took a photo and we moved on.

The Spanish monarchy had once used Buen Retiro Park as their private retreat, but in the late nineteenth century they turned it over to the people of the city. It was now full of commoners strolling arm in arm, wandering with ice-creams, and so, because of the passing trade, tall black men selling fake sunglasses or bags on large white sheets abounded.

Angela and I stopped at the edge of a large lake. Blue and white rowing boats were sloshing around in the middle while ducks ducked and dived around at the edge. Below them were shoals of silvery-grey fish. A young couple just along from us were feeding them bits of bread.

"I've been thinking," said Angela. "When we go to France tomorrow, we should hire a car."

I didn't comment. I was feeling at peace with the world. Parks had the power to do that, I'd noticed, especially ones with lakes.

Angela continued. "With a car, we can see a few different places. Drive around and see a bit of the Dordogne in between. It's meant to be beautiful. You know how much I love rustic French villages. What do you think?"

I was watching a duck attacking a piece of bread that the young couple had thrown in the water. Its flat beak quickly demolished it. "Good idea."

That settled, we walked further into the park until we came across a gigantic glass building known as the Crystal Palace. Originally constructed to house exotic plants from the Orient, it was empty, save for a small art exhibition and a group of noisy children. After perusing a few pictures, we stood outside, wondering what to do next.

"The airport?" Angela asked.

I looked at my watch and nodded. Time had flashed by in Madrid. We journeyed back to the hotel, packed our bags and, this time around, managed to get on the correct train to the airport without any mishaps whatsoever. Madrid had been fun, we both agreed, but now it was time to head to France, and not to the obvious choice of Paris, but to Bordeaux, in the south west. Unlike my earlier visit to France, when it had been a mere stopover on the way to Monaco, this time we were going to see France in all its glory.

Top row: The Royal Palace; An archway leading off from Plaza Mayor
Middle row: Busy street in downtown Madrid; A rather portly Spiderman; Supposedly the oldest restaurant in the world
Bottom row: City Hall; One of the graceful buildings in Plaza Mayor

Chapter 17. Bordeaux, France

Interesting fact: It is illegal to call a French pig Napoleon.

Our arrival at Bordeaux Airport went without incident. One hour later, during the evening rush hour, the incident occurred. Angela and I were sitting in the hire car on a motorway exit road causing pure mayhem.

"The bloody clutch pedal is stuck," I shrieked as I tried to get the car to engage first gear. "I can't move it."

Underneath my foot, the pedal seemed glued to the floor and there was nothing I could do except curse. In the rear view mirror, a snarl of traffic was building up. From somewhere came an angry beep, and then another. Ten seconds later, a driver managed to squeeze past by overtaking on the main motorway, a dangerous manoeuvre by any measure. Another driver followed his lead, and, as he passed, he mouthed something to me. I got the impression it wasn't anything nice. I tried yanking the gear stick forward with pure might, but it refused to budge a millimetre.

"Do something," said Angela.

"What do you think I'm doing? I snapped. "Sitting here for fun?" I stomped down hard on the pedal and yanked on the gear stick again. "What's wrong with it?"

And then, as if it had toyed with us enough, the clutch pedal came up. I pressed it down and engaged the gear. It smoothly slid into place and I gingerly lifted the clutch. We moved off, finally able to leave the motorway of doom.

2

Twenty hellish minutes later, we found our hotel. Though the car had behaved for the remainder of the journey, I'd lost all trust in it and parked the thing with relief. After dropping off our bags, we got a taxi into the centre of the city.

Within a few minutes, the grandeur of Bordeaux's riverfront buildings came into view. Bordeaux looked *rich*, and, by the time we reached the city centre and stopped, I wished we were rich. The taxi driver pointed to the almost-hidden meter, which read twenty-four euros. I passed him twenty-five and received no change. We climbed out, wondering how a thousand mile journey in a jet aircraft could be cheaper than a six-minute journey in a taxi.

We were both pleasantly surprised by Bordeaux, though. It was beautiful and well cared for. The buildings were stately, the pavements polished, the boutique stores chic and every woman, young and old, was elegantly fashionable in a way that only the French could pull off. We walked along a wide boulevard until we came to a restaurant with a set of outdoor tables.

The menu, of course, was in French, but we had come somewhat prepared. For a few months, we'd listened to CDs that taught us basic French, hopefully enough to get by. However, after only two or three CDs, it became clear that Angela was picking up the language far better than I was. She could understand the nuances of grammar and punctuation, while I was still stuck on phrases involving childish innuendo.

"Bonjour!" said the waitress. "Voulez-vous voir la menu?"

I looked at Angela. I got the bonjour bit, but the rest was gobbledygook. Angela smiled. "Oui," she replied, "je voudrais une bouteille de vin rouge, s'il vous plait, avec deux verre!" The waitress nodded and wandered away.

"What did she say and what did you say back? You actually sounded French."

"She asked if we wanted to see the menu, and I said yes. Then I ordered a bottle of red wine with two glasses."

The red wine Angela ordered was lovely, and after she inspected the label, she informed me it was from the chateau.

"Is that important?" I asked with a hint of a French accent. If I couldn't speak the lingo, at least I could do a fair impression of it.

"It means it was bottled at the chateau where the vineyards are. It's usually a good sign."

The meal I ordered was thin strips of raw beef with the added bonus of a pickled artichoke to choke on. It wasn't what I'd expected, of course, but it looked suitably French and so I was happy. Angela's food was much nicer, but then she had understood the menu.

Later, we found a lively square surrounded by cafes and bars. Many of the surrounding buildings had flower arrangements set up on their windowsills. It was all deliciously pretty. While I supped a pint of Meteor lager, a quartet of young men began setting up for some sort of street performance. Soon, some tinny music started and they began to dance. It was a modern piece, complete with handstands and impressive jiving, and then, when the song finished, the four of them went literally cap in hand. It was a nice way to end our first evening in France.

3

The next day, we checked out of the hotel and climbed in the hire car. Our next stop was Perigueux, two hours east from Bordeaux. To be honest, I'd never heard of Perigueux, but Angela had, telling me it was a gorgeous little town that we simply had to visit. Luckily, the car was behaving itself and when we passed the outskirts of Bordeaux and French countryside began to fill the view, I calmed down.

We travelled between vineyards and rustic French villages straight out of *Allo Allo*. All they needed were thick-moustachioed men riding bicycles, with strings of onions dangling over their handlebars, and the scenes would be complete. We arrived in Perigueux by early afternoon. The sun was shining, the sky a perfect azure and our French odyssey was in phase two of its operation.

4

Two thousand years previously, the Romans built amphitheatres, artesian wells, villas and temples that could accommodate 20,000 people in a settlement called Vesunna. This eventually became Perigueux. As Angela and I crossed the cobblestone streets of the compact city centre, we couldn't see any evidence of the Romans, but we could see lots of medieval architecture, including the magnificent Cathedral St-Front, a white-grey building whose tower rose like a sentinel. Opposite it, a small bookshop proudly boasted that it sold *Livres: anciens & moderns.* It was closed, and so we walked on until we came to an alleyway with nail-studded wooden doors. With a cart and horse, and perhaps a man carrying a broadsword, the side streets of Perigueux would have made a wonderful backdrop for any period drama of the Middle Ages.

"Bonjour!" said the proprietor of a local wine shop, a man in his sixties with a close crop of white hair, as we entered his store.

"Bonjour!" I replied, my accent superb and my diction spot on. And then he started speaking at a hundred miles an hour and I didn't understand a word of it. It was like being in the underground museum in Luxembourg all over again. Judging by Angela's expression, she hadn't understood him either, but she was pretending to look at a bottle of wine.

"Parlez-vous Anglais?" I asked hopefully.

The man shook his head. I shrugged, smiled, and then joined Angela. The man watched us, seemingly sorry he couldn't tell us about his wares, but the prices were already putting us off – every bottle was way out of our price range. We pretended to read a few more labels, nodding thoughtfully and headed for the door.

"Au revoir," the man said jovially.

Angela was already stepping out of the exit and so it was down to me to reply. "Bonjour!" I boomed, pleased with my swift response. The man looked confused, and then said bonjour back. I closed the door as Angela burst out laughing.

~ 190 ~

Our one and only evening in Perigueux was spent having a lovely meal in yet another outdoor cafe. Just across from us, market stalls were tempting evening browsers with their cheeses, wines and ornaments. From somewhere came the sound of a brass band.

"I think I could live here," said Angela.

"I think I could, too. And it's not often I say that. Here or Monaco, or maybe Reykjavik."

Angela picked up her glass of wine. After taking a sip, she looked around at the square. It was bustling but calm. Everyone seemed happy with their lot in Perigueux, and for a moment I could imagine ourselves living among these folk, buying baguettes in the morning and sipping wine in the evening. Perigueux had caught us in its spell.

5

The next morning, we were on the road again. We had a three-hour journey to Royan, a small seaside resort north of Bordeaux. Along the way, we passed fields full of grapes and sunflowers. The roads were long and we were making good time.

Feeling peckish, we stopped for lunch. It turned out to be another gorgeous little French village, complete with a gentle river, cobbled streets, ancient abbey, and, best of all, cafes and patisseries to satiate our hungry palates. We were in Brantome, on a meander in the Dronne Valley. After a croissant and a cafe au lait, we wandered around, coming across another shop selling wine. Prepared this time, Angela did all the talking, and luckily the woman spoke a little English. We left with a couple of bottles of the region's finest.

We arrived in Royan an hour later. The blue skies of the previous two days had made way for clouds, with even a spot of rain on the horizon.

Royan, we learned, had suffered during the Second World War. German troops had occupied key sectors of the town, and so three hundred and fifty RAF bombers were sent there on a cold January morning in 1945 to obliterate the town, believing it to be free of civilians. It wasn't, and a thousand innocents were killed. Worse came the next day, this time from a fleet of American bombers. As well as carrying traditional bombs, the US planes were transporting napalm (the highly flammable mixture of gelling agent and fuel that stuck to anything it came into contact with, including human skin), which they dropped over Royan with devastating effect. This time, 1700 more civilians were killed. If this tragic event had occurred in 1980, it would have been classed as a war crime, but, back in 1945, it was simply an effective tool against the enemy. These attacks in Royan paved the way for heavier napalm use in Asia against the Japanese, and then, later still, in the Korean and Vietnam wars. The net result for Royan, however, was that it no longer existed. When the Allies realised what they had done, they were understandably horrified and offered to pay for a complete rebuild. So today, instead of being a quaint Victorian-themed seaside town, Royan is a purpose-built 1950s sprawl.

6

As with most places that have seen unimaginable horror, it was hard to find any evidence of what had happened. There were no buildings with bullet holes and no memorials to those who had lost their lives, at least as far as we could see. But there were lots of teenagers surfing, pensioners playing games of bowls in specially constructed sand enclosures near the beach and pedestrians ambling along the sea front

Now that the sun had come out, Royan seemed a universe away from what it must have looked like in the dark days of January 1945, but it no one would describe it as a pretty town. Faded hotels, lacklustre walkways and old benches whitewashed with seagull droppings gave the town a look far from its best. Angela and I walked along the front, following a young couple pushing a pram. They stopped to look in a gift shop that sold the same touristy fare (postcards, sunglasses, buckets and spades) as their British counterparts, and we overtook them. After realising there wasn't much else to do, we turned around and made our way onto the beach towards a set of blue and white-striped deck chairs. After paying for a couple, we flopped out, idly watching a banner-towing light aircraft overhead, its distant engines almost drowning out the occasional round of polite applause from the pensioners playing bowls. For two hours we sat and did nothing. It was a fine way to recharge our batteries after a hectic week of West European travel.

In the car the next morning, we passed through a part of Royan we had not seen – the better side: yachts and sailing boats filling up a lively and pretty harbour.

"Sod's law," I said. Beside me, Angela nodded. But we had no time to stop, because we needed to get back to Bordeaux so we could drop the hire car off. Next stop was Ireland. It would involve another short transfer through Gatwick, but we could live with that if it meant seeing a little bit of the Emerald Isle.

Top row: Bordeaux old town; A bottle of red wine – from the chateau
Middle row: Angela enjoying the café culture of France; The village of Brantome
Bottom row: Perigueux Cathedral; a busy beach in Royan

Chapter 18. Cork, Ireland

Interesting fact: Ireland has won the Eurovision Song Contest more times than any other country.

"Sweet bloody Jesus and Christ almighty!" came the voice of the man behind us. These were the first words Angela and I heard upon our arrival at Cork International Airport. What caused the man to utter these words we did not know, but it cheered us nonetheless. We had arrived in Ireland and it sounded good.

The wonderfully named Saint Finbarr founded Cork in the sixth century. He established a monastery that proved so popular that people began to build their homes near it; when even more folk did the same, the settlement turned into a village and then a small town. But things took a turn for the worse when some ships arrived from the freezing north. The ships were full of angry bearded folk who called themselves the Norsemen. They rampaged through Cork, razing much of it to the ground as they pillaged their way along the Irish coastline. But the Vikings didn't destroy it all, and over time, they even began to appreciate Cork. They liked it enough to turn the town into some sort of trading post. So despite the initial damage, Cork began to prosper.

The Viking ships eventually left and the Black Death came. It wiped out half of Cork's population. By the seventeenth century, however, Cork finally hit the big time. It became the butter capital of the world, providing the foodstuff to ships plying the busy transatlantic routes. People in Cork became rich on the back of their butter production. But the good times did not last. The infamous potato famine of the mid-nineteenth century, followed by British interference, drove the city into decline. It would take until the mid-1990s for Ireland's second largest city to fully recover.

2

"So where-yas-from?" asked the jovial taxi driver as we left the airport. In his sixties and wearing a blue sailor's cap, he looked like an old sea dog. When we told him we were from England, he visibly cheered.

"Ah, England! I do love that place! Lived in Liverpool many years ago. And before dat, in Birmingham, so I did!"

Heading into the city, Angela and I surveyed our surroundings. We had expected Cork to be a picture-postcard sort of town, perhaps a bit like Whitby, but so far it seemed to be stuck in some sort of weird time warp, alternating between run-down Victorian buildings and drab 60s-style blocks. A closed-down cinema added to this effect, the fly posters and graffiti adorning its once grand entrance making it look distinctly uninviting.

"Cobh is a nice place if you have the time," said the taxi driver, perhaps sensing our mood. "It's got a lovely little harbour. It was the final port where the Titanic stopped before setting off across the Atlantic. It's about half an hour by bus. As well as Cobh, there's Blarney, of course. You've got to kiss the stone!"

We told him we would try. "Out of interest," I asked, "what's the Murphy's like here?" Irish stout was a favourite of mine. I'd tried Guinness in Dublin once and now I wanted to try Murphy's in Cork, the place it was brewed.

"Oh, they all taste the same to me," the man answered honestly. "I like a good whisky myself, but the wife likes a bit of stout now and again. She says the Guinness doesn't travel too well, so she prefers the Murphy's."

"I might stick to the Murphy's then," I said.

Not long after, the man dropped us off outside the hotel and wished us a pleasant time in Cork.

3

The next morning was overcast and drizzly: typical Irish weather. Our hotel, located on a high hill to the north of the River Lee, was full of shuddering lifts and long stark corridors. "It says here," I said, reading a placard on a wall, "that this place used to be a hospital for people with incurable diseases. Maybe there are still traces of disease in the beds."

"What sorts of diseases?"

"Mainly typhoid, tuberculosis and cholera. The locals still call this place the Fever Hospital."

"Ooh! Sounds like an episode from *Scooby Doo*."

After breakfast, we headed into the city centre to begin our sightseeing trek. It quickly led us to the main shopping district, an area crisscrossed by St Patrick's Street, Oliver Plunkett Street and the Grand Parade. Our first port of call was the English Market, a seventeenth century set of indoor stalls selling meat, fish, cheese, bread and lots more besides.

The aroma inside was definitely *meaty*, but that was because we had entered near the meat section. Further in, we passed stalls with names like Moynihans Poultry and O'Connel Seafood; all of them were busy with customers. The jovial sound of early-morning conversation filled the hall; it seemed a jolly place and I could see why Queen Elizabeth II had enjoyed a browse during her state visit to Ireland in 2011.

Back outside, the view to the north of the River Lee wasn't particularly picturesque. It looked like any other industrial city. Drab buildings, grey listless housing, tall red-brick chimneys and a set of gaudy shop fronts greeted our gaze as we headed towards a bridge.

"I thought Cork was supposed to be beautiful," I said, looking at the grim skyline. "This is like a scene L.S. Lowry would paint."

Angela pulled out the guidebook. The front cover photograph showed row upon row of brightly coloured houses on the side of the steep hill. In front of them was the Atlantic Ocean lapping up against a sea wall. Cork wasn't anywhere near the ocean, and there were no colourful buildings that we could see. I took the guidebook and turned to the first page. In small print at the bottom, it said the front cover photo was of Cobh (pronounced Cove), the nearby coastal town the taxi driver had mentioned.

"That's a bit cheeky, isn't it?" said Angela.

"Yeah. It's like having a photo of a Rolls Royce outside the garage but having a Ford Escort inside."

Angela smiled. "It's not quite as bad as that."

We walked on until we came to the bridge. After traversing the wide grey river, we headed uphill towards the Firkin Crane Centre.

4

A firkin is an old measurement of mass, with one firkin being equivalent to about 25 kilograms. The Firkin Crane Centre used to be part of Cork's Butter Exchange. In the mid nineteenth century, butter was weighed on specially made scales called cranes before being sent on its way to markets across the world. When Cork's butter heydays ended, the owners of the circular building decided to make margarine instead, but, by the 1970s, even that was old hat, and so the building was left deserted. And that's perhaps how it would have stayed had it not been for a group of forward-thinking business people who secured funds to refurbish it. Instead of being a hotbed of dairy manufacture, the Firkin Crane Centre reinvented itself as a venue for contemporary dance.

"I'm not being funny," said Angela, "but why have you brought me here?" We were standing outside the entrance. Posters of dancers in strange poses were near the door.

"To see some contemporary dancing. Maybe even join in with some. Apparently we can have lessons."

Angela laughed. "What's the real reason?"

I pointed to another building. "That."

Angela looked a bit further down the street and read the sign. "A butter museum? You actually want to go in a museum? About butter. Really?"

"I want to prove I'm not the heathen you think I am. We're in Cork. Cork is famous for butter. I think we should find out what it's all about. Besides, the guidebook describes the museum as unmissable. Look..." I flicked through the guidebook to show her.

Angela read it and then studied me for a moment. "You *really* want to go in?"

"Yeah, come on."

5

After paying the entrance fee, we watched a short video detailing the butter making process, and how the brand *Kerrygold* came into being. It was all highly boring, but I pretended I was interested. Later, in a display room, I regarded a wooden barrel for a few moments, and then read the information sign next to it. I made sure I read every word and then stared at the barrel again, rubbing my chin thoughtfully.

Next, I stared at some sort of churning implement. Again, I studied the artefact from every angle possible, and then made a show of reading the information sign. As soon as I'd finished, I realised I couldn't remember a single word. It didn't matter though, because I read it again.

"I know what you're doing," whispered Angela.

"Shush. I'm trying to read."

"You're pretending to be interested when I know for a fact you're not."

I looked at the black churning barrel and angled my head slightly, as if considering how to make butter myself. I could tell Angela was itching to move on, but I was in no rush. I looked back at the display and started to read it for a third time.

"Oh, for heaven's sake," muttered Angela. "Stop pretending. I admit defeat. I'm as bad as you are. I'm a museum heathen. Let's go."

I smiled and accepted the admission. We raced through the remainder of the butter-making artefacts and were outside five minutes later. Across the street was Saint Anne's Shandon Church.

6

Saint Anne's is famous in Cork because of its eight bells. A nineteenth century poet wrote a poem about them, which people liked, and so people started to come to see the bells for themselves.

We entered the church and found a kindly woman inside, who told us it was five euros each to climb the tower. "But be careful," she warned in her warm Irish brogue. "The steps are a bit on the rickety side at the moment. I wouldn't like you to slip and hurt yerselves. But you'll enjoy the view from the top, I'm sure. And make sure you ring the bells on the way up."

"Is anyone else up there?" I asked.

The woman shook her head. "No, it's been a quiet day today. Just you and the ghosts."

We thanked the woman and set off. The steps were both steep and indeed rickety; at the half way stage, we came to a small platform where the famous bells ropes were. Eight of them hung there, each with its own number. Someone had produced a few laminated cards with songs written on them. I picked up one card and Angela began pulling the numbered ropes in the right order, tentatively playing a song called *The Last Rose of Summer*. From above our heads somewhere, the bells chimed, a loud reverberating clanging that shook the roof. I didn't recognise the tune though. Angela tried another song called *The Derry Air*, which we didn't recognise either.

"There should be songs like *It's a Long Way to Tipperary* or *Danny Boy* on these cards, songs that people recognise. Come on," I said. "Enough of this malarkey."

At the next platform, there were some large padded headphones dangling from a rafter. Above them were the eight bells of

Shandon. While we stared up at them, they suddenly kicked into cacophonous life, swinging and then causing massive vibrations, which threatened to burst our eardrums.

"Jesus!" I yelled. "Grab some headphones. Quick."

We did so and the noise became just about bearable. Evidently, someone below us was playing a tune. It was the Tune from Hell. I looked at Angela. She looked ridiculous wearing the ear defenders, but then I probably did too. As the bells continued to clang and bang, shaking the walls, we noticed a little door with more steps leading upwards. We followed them, squeezing over some rafters into a narrow opening. After some furious climbing, we found ourselves outside. We removed our headphones.

As we looked over a grey and misty Cork, the bells became quiet. We could see the river in the distance, surrounded by a mixture of Victorian and post-war buildings, with the occasional church spire poking above them. Angela nudged me. "What's it called again? You know, bell ringing?"

I thought for a moment. "Campanology, I think. Why? Are you thinking of joining a group when we get home?"

Just then, a young man appeared, and his girlfriend popped up behind him – the phantom bell ringers. After we all nodded at each other, they moved to a section of viewing point a bit further along from us and we decided to head back down. When we reached the rope platform, I toyed with the idea of waiting for the young couple to arrive under the bells. I'd noticed they were not wearing headphones, and, if I timed it just right, they would get a taste of their own noisy medicine. Angela told me to stop being so childish and so we carried on to the bottom.

7

A visit to Cork without seeing the Blarney Stone would have been a travesty of travel justice. We hopped on a bus for the twenty-minute journey to the little town of Blarney, only eight kilometres northwest of Cork.

Blarney village was certainly prettier than Cork. Instead of mainly grey and white buildings, the townsfolk of Blarney had painted theirs in pastel pinks, blues and oranges, and had built a small grassy square in the centre of town, a place swarming with tourists, mostly American. Seven or eight coaches were parked nearby, but, apart from a few people browsing the gift shops or entering the orange Muskerry Arms, everyone was walking towards the prime attraction – the six-hundred year old Blarney Castle.

The castle stood in the grounds of a large area of parkland. After paying the twelve euro entrance fee, we crossed over a small bridge towards it. Below, in the stream, were hundreds of coins, tossed over the side for good luck. I threw one in myself, making a secret wish that I would one day be a millionaire and own a helicopter.

"What did you wish for?" asked Angela.

"I'm not telling you or it won't come true."

Angela looked at me. "Come on. Tell me."

"Okay, fine. I wished that we will grow old together and still have our faculties intact."

Angela looked at me and pulled a face. "As if you wished for that."

The castle was made of bluestone, a variety of limestone noted for its bluish hue. Its main section was tall and rectangular with bits missing from its turrets, as if siege weapons had attacked it. A few smaller, circular towers made of grey stone stood nearby, all of them in a similar state of ruin. Woodland and foliage surrounded the castle, with pathways leading all around. We passed a sign pointing to something called the Druid's Circle and Witch's Cave. We ignored them and entered the castle, climbing the spiralling stone staircase. After only a few steps we found ourselves at the back of a queue.

Elderly Americans were in front and soon some more were behind us. The steps were thick with American chatter. We were all in line to kiss the famous stone, supposed to bring eloquence to anyone who did so. Every so often we would shuffle up a couple of steps, with an air of expectancy that we might be nearing the top, only to come to another standstill.

"Don't get mad," whispered Angela. She knew my threshold for queue waiting was dangerously short. "Because there's nothing we can do."

I nodded as we moved another couple of steps upwards, waiting behind the American couple who were discussing their trip around Ireland. It sounded like they had been all over the place, but their favourite was Galway. Finally, we emerged onto a small battlement. The queue continued, but at least now we could see daylight.

The top of the castle was square shaped, with a flat platform running around each edge. At the front of the queue was a woman going through the process of kissing the Blarney Stone. We watched carefully so we would know what to do. First the woman lay down on her back, while the kindly gentleman in charge held onto her in case she slipped. If she did, there was a good chance she could fall onto the metal grille below, which would be undoubtedly embarrassing and painful. Better than falling to her death, though: below the grille was nothing but thin air and then the ground. By now, the woman was stretching her neck forward to kiss the stone. Somehow she accomplished this feat and stood up, looking proud of herself. Now it was time for her husband, and the whole process was repeated.

We shuffled forwards with the rest of the queue, edging towards the front of the line until it was our turn. As I prepared myself, the man in charge got up and started fiddling with a flask on a nearby wall. "Ah," he said to us. "I'm just having a tea break! I won't be long. Ten minutes is all I'll be. I just need to wet my whistle."

I turned to Angela, wondering what she wanted to do. Personally, I was happy to give the whole kissing thing a miss. I'd seen the stone, I'd photographed the stone, but kissing the stone was something I could leave for another day. Quite frankly, it looked like something only a simpleton would want to do. Plus, I might get mud on my back. I said all this to Angela while the man in charge sipped his tea out of earshot. Angela agreed and so we stepped past the rather plain-looking Blarney Stone and clambered down another spiralling stone staircase.

8

"Well that was firkin fun," I said as we left the grounds of the castle. "But I think it's time for a pint of Beamish."

O'Connor's Muskerry Arms sold all three kinds of stout, and was packed to the rafters with locals and tourists alike. Angela and I sat down in a corner so I could enjoy a pint of Beamish Stout. To be perfectly honest, Guinness, Murphy's and Beamish all looked identical to me, and they tasted similar too. That said, the Beamish I was currently sipping was a mighty fine drink, and, while Angela settled down to look at some shoes she'd bought in a shop around the corner, I leafed through a magazine I'd found. One page caught my eye. It was an advertisement for an upcoming play to be shown in Cork. Its rather mundane name, *Cleaner*, couldn't have prepared me for what I was about to read. The blurb read like something out of a Monty Python script. *'Using a combination of puppetry, dance and domestic cleaning products'*, it read, *'Cleaner is an alternative adult fairytale about a woman who falls in love with her sweeping brush.'* I gulped a mouthful of Beamish down.

"Do you think," asked Angela, "we are the first people to visit the Blarney Stone and not kiss it?"

I thought about this. It did seem an odd thing to do: get a bus to Blarney, walk to the castle, pay the entrance fee, climb the tower, wait in a long queue to kiss it and then, when it was our turn, simply walk away. "Probably."

"I wonder what the man thought."

"Probably thought we were eejits."

"Maybe we are. In fact, if anyone asks, I think we should say we did kiss it. It'll be embarrassing otherwise."

"Agreed."

I finished my stout and we headed outside to catch a bus back to Cork.

9

For our final morning in Cork, we decided to walk to St Finbarre's Cathedral, south of the river this time. Walking through the main thoroughfare of shopping streets, we were once again struck by just how drab the city looked; even the sun couldn't bring any sparkle to the place. But then, as we passed the massive Beamish Brewery, things began to look better. With the small tributary of the River Lee on our right, this was perhaps the most picturesque part of the city we'd seen, especially with the yellow and maroon townhouses on the left, and the spires of St Finbarre's poking upwards.

The cathedral was at the end of a leafy stone lane, and, like Blarney Castle, it looked like it had been constructed from bluestone. The gates leading to it appeared locked, and there sounded like there was some sort of service going on. Instead of going in we stood at the railings, looking at the triple spires, and a golden statue of an angel.

"Well, I've enjoyed Cork," I said as we turned tail. It was time to return to the Fever Hospital to pack our bags. "I know it's been a bit drab, but everyone's been really friendly, and there was enough for us to do, I think."

"I'm ready to go home though. This constant: airport – hotel – airport – hotel is tiring me out. I don't know how you do it by yourself for so long."

"By myself is easy. If I get tired, I just go to sleep. If I fancy a hotdog, I buy a hotdog. With you, I've got to think about what you might want to do, or where you might want to eat; it's not as easy."

"Charming."

"No, you know what I mean. Anyway, I'm ready to go home too. I'm worn out."

A few hours later, as we sat aboard the Aer Lingus flight to Manchester, I reflected on our travels to Western Europe so far. Including Ireland, I'd been to nineteen different countries, and Angela had been to nine. Not bad going considering, I'd visited them all in just two separate trips. But our summer travels had to end for the time being. Work beckoned, as did saving up again. We would resume our journey in the winter, where I would be kicking things off with a solo jaunt to San Marino.

*Top left: Panorama of Cork, looking out towards Saint Fin
Barre's Cathedral; A pint of Beamish
Middle row: Angela ringing the bells of Saint Anne's; Muskerry
Arms, Blarney; The spire of Saint Anne's
Bottom row: Blarney Castle; Street in central Cork*

Part 3

San Marino, Austria, Germany, Finland

Chapter 19. San Marino, San Marino

Interesting fact: San Marino is the oldest republic in the world.

San Marino is another of the world's microstates. Like Liechtenstein, Andorra, the Vatican and Monaco, it exists in a bizarre state of independence, issuing its own stamps, having its own government and even possessing its own army, even though in all but name it is part of another country – in this case, Italy. San Marino is surrounded by Italy, and the people who live there speak Italian, spend the same currency (the euro) and travel between both nations as if no border exists.

According to legend, a Croatian stonemason called Marinus founded San Marino in the year 301. Marinus was a committed Christian who, to escape persecution in his homeland, sailed to Italy and settled in the Italian town of Rimini. There he downed his hammers and chisels and became a priest, rising to the rank of bishop. But trouble was just around the corner for Marinus. It came in the form of an insane woman who claimed that the bishop was her husband. No one believed it, of course, but the woman's constant hounding sent Marinus running to the hills. Literally. He built himself a chapel on top of Mount Titanus, and some people followed him; before he knew it, a community developed. By the ninth century, San Marino became an official city state, and, due to its relative inaccessibility, on top of a mountain, and the fact that it was hardly a political or economic heavyweight anyway, the country managed to cling onto independence while other city states (the Republic of Venice and the Republic of Genoa, most notably) became incorporated into Italy.

2

Getting to the fifth-smallest country in the world was more difficult than I thought it would be. First, I had to fly to Copenhagen, and wait for four hours before boarding another SAS flight to the Italian city of Bologna. From Bologna airport, I caught a bus into town and booked myself into the hotel nearest to the central train station. After that, I grabbed a slice of pizza and a couple of beers and then went to bed. It had been a long day.

The next morning was pleasantly sunny – an ideal December day for visiting a new country. It was also freezing, and so I grabbed a warming coffee and crossed the road to the train station. After securing my first class return ticket to the coastal town of Rimini (it was only a few euros more than the second-class ticket), I sat on the platform and waited.

I knew next to nothing about San Marino, except that it had an international football team and a Formula 1 racing circuit. I also knew that the race circuit was not actually in San Marino, but in Italy. A movement to my left attracted my attention. It was a couple of obese people attacking a platform vending machine. The woman was jabbing her finger on the part that returned coins while her partner, a large man with a backpack, shook the machine, his breath spilling out like an enraged beast. Back and forth it rocked, but it would not offer any chocolate, sweets or crisps. The man bellowed and shook it again while his companion glared and breathed fire. But it was no use: breakfast would not be served that morning.

Ten minutes later, a train pulled up at the platform. All around, people were furiously puffing on cigarettes. It was as if the last hour of the cigarette smoker had been declared, and the platform was thick with smoke. I sidestepped the smokers and found my first-class seat: number 13. It wasn't as luxurious as I'd hoped, but at least it was comfortable and there was nobody sitting next to me. I settled back for the hour's journey to Rimini.

3

Opposite me sat a middle-aged couple. As we set off, I caught the man's eye and nodded. He returned the gesture and then looked out of the window. I did too, staring blankly at the graffiti and the buildings beyond.

Bologna was supposedly a beautiful city, the seventh largest in Italy no less, but all I could see was ugly concrete and nothing much else. A few minutes later, the train lurched to a stop at a small station. A few passengers boarded, including an elderly Italian gentleman. The man was angry and the source of his ire was me.

"Stupido idiota!" the man hissed, causing people to look. The friendly couple opposite looked shocked. The pensioner, who looked remarkably like the man on the front of Dolmio jars, carried on ranting in thick Italian.

I raised my hands at the sudden outburst. "I can't understand what you're saying. Can you speak English?"

The man sneered and let rip again. I was now the centre of attention in the whole carriage. First class it may have been, but with an Englishman on board, it had been reduced to a chav estate. I didn't know what to do, barring throwing myself (or him) out of the window, and so I showed the old man my ticket, pointing at the number 13. This brought a fresh wave of abuse in my direction.

"Please stop," I said. "I don't know what you're saying. Unless you can speak English, I suggest you sit in this seat." I gestured to the seat empty next to me. The man looked and then unleashed another wave of volatile Italian. It was as if I had smeared his homestead in excrement and then had kicked his pet dog in the eye. The whole scene was ridiculous to the extreme.

"Excuse me," said a voice to my left. It belonged to a man in a suit. "I'm afraid you *are* sitting in this man's seat. Seat 13 is an aisle seat. You are in number 12."

I looked at my ticket and then at the overhead graphic showing which seat was which. I sighed. So I was in the wrong. I stood up and moved out into the aisle, allowing my tormentor to squeeze by. As he did so, the man in the suit gave me a pained expression, as if to say, 'Sorry about this.' As for the old swine, he was as snug as a git in a pile of horse manure. He'd beaten the foreigner into submission and was now wallowing in the window seat of his glory.

4

Rimini was less than thrilling out of season, but then again, I only saw the area around the train station. Pigeons ruled the rafters while white camper vans ruled the roads and parking spaces. I milled around for a bit, hovering near a Burger King, then grew bored so walked around the block, hands thrust into my pockets. There wasn't much to see, so I returned to the front of Burger King to wait for the bus. It wasn't due to arrive for another thirty minutes so I bought a coffee, more to warm my hands than anything.

Other passengers arrived, all foreigners by the sound of them. There was a trio of young Russian girls, all lipstick and high heels, a couple of Chinese women and a lone middle-aged Japanese man. Then a group of middle-aged Germans arrived. The bus was going to be full of international passengers.

Five minutes late, the modern San Marino bus pulled up and we all boarded. Nine euros for a round trip up a mountain and back seemed like good value, and soon we were heading through the outskirts of Rimini, passing Tamoil petrol stations and empty vineyards. At one point, close to the San Marino border, we passed a collection of planes perched on a hilltop. An old jet fighter, a small turboprop passenger aircraft, a helicopter and what looked like a World War 1 biplane were all sitting on the side of the hill. A large sign read *Museo dell'Aviazione*. I stared at the planes, wondering how on earth the owners had got them up there.

As expected, crossing the border between Italy and San Marino was a simple matter of driving along a road. There was no border as such, and the only reason I knew we had crossed was because of a sign saying *San Marino*. Up in the distance, almost in silhouette, were the cliff-top castles of San Marino City, the capital of the tiny nation. They stood upon Mount Titano, and to get there we had to pass through San Marino's biggest town – Dogana, home of large shopping centres and something called the Medieval Store, which was full to the brim with broadswords, axes and metal knight costumes.

I quickly surmised that San Marino was identical in almost every way to Italy. The only difference was the distinctive blue and white car number plates. I sat back as we traversed a series of hairpin bends towards our goal.

5

The coach dropped us off in a large car park, flanked by a high stone wall at one end and a set of gift shops at the other. There were seven or eight empty coaches already parked, and, as we climbed out, a tourist train snaked its way around the corner. Christmas music was blaring from its speakers.

A lot of tourists were standing outside the shops. I wandered over to them, noticing the middle-aged Japanese man was already hot-footing it up some steps to the main part of town. He looked like a man on a mission. The shops were selling key rings, chocolate bars, flags and bottles of Titanbrau, San Marino's national beer. The displays showed lots of Cyrillic, an indicator of how many Russians visited the nation. I decided to follow the lead of the Japanese man and climbed the steps. At the top was another steep path, which opened into a shopping arcade. The man was nowhere to be seen, and so I wandered around the cafes, bars and gun shops. Yes, gun shops. I was shocked to learn San Marino had the most relaxed gun laws in Europe, meaning submachine guns, revolvers and all sorts of pistols could be purchased, as could a vast array of knives and crossbows. Why anyone would want to purchase such weaponry was beyond me, but every gunsmith was packed.

I walked to a high wall and looked out across the landscape. Beyond a nearby church spire was a rolling series of peaks and valleys, some shrouded in mist. It was a scene befitting a dragon. As if on cue, I heard a woman cackling. It was coming from above so I turned around to see. On another high-turreted wall, ten or twelve people were gazing downwards. None looked like a witch, but then I heard it again – a high-pitched, authentically accurate, hag-like cackle. And then I spotted her. It was a woman with blonde hair. She was looking directly at me, or at least I thought so. Then she was gone.

I decided to search out the torture museum. My guidebook suggested that San Marino's torture museum was supposed to be rather good, featuring a whole range of historical torture equipment. I ambled around the winding streets of the town for a while, hoping to stumble across it, and, after wandering past even more gun shops, I finally spied a sign saying *Museo Delle Cere Strumenti Tortura 30m*, and, underneath, *Not to be missed!*

I found the entrance and paid my seven euros in eager anticipation.

6

In Bratislava, capital of Slovakia, I'd visited a torture museum. I'd been horrified at some of the implements on show, and then mesmerised by some of the gruesome pictures. I was expecting more of the same inside San Marino's torture museum, but soon came to realise that I would be sorely disappointed. For a start, the vast majority of the waxworks on offer were not being tortured. Instead, they were poor representations of famous people in totally unconvincing poses: Abraham Lincoln, Napoleon Bonaparte, Benito Mussolini, Adolf Hitler and plenty of other people I didn't know stood inside darkened rooms. I sped past them, hoping to come across something more interesting.

Around a corner, I came across a waxwork of a man being hanged. Finally a bit of the good stuff. I peered at the figure closely, noticing he looked like a shop mannequin. Someone had flopped a shiny black wig over his head, dressed him in historic clothes and then placed him in a noose. It was a pathetic attempt at terror, and I wasn't surprised I was the only person inside the museum.

In another display, a man wearing red velvet trousers was sitting down while another man pressed a wooden beam down onto his knees. The beam had long nails sticking out of it, and I could well imagine the terrible pain they would have caused had they been real. But the waxwork victim's expression was neutral, as was his torturer's, which negated the effect somewhat. There was no agony or pain on the face, only a standard expression. In fact, all the waxworks in the whole museum seemed to have the same face, and I wondered whether they had obtained a job lot of store dolls and had simply dressed them up. It really was that bad. I left soon after, wondering how the guidebook had got it so wrong. As I passed the man who had sold me the ticket, I noticed he had the decency to look a little embarrassed.

7

San Marino was fairy-tale pretty. It was full of fortified stony walls, sky-reaching battlements and musicians wandering around playing festive tunes. I walked by stalls selling roasted chestnuts and fragrant-smelling mead until I came to one of the old towers. Dating from the eleventh century, it looked like something from a fantasy film. I could picture fair maidens and court jesters quivering inside its towers while fire-breathing dragons rumbled overhead.

"I'm not going to tell you again, Lucy," said a voice belonging to an American woman. She was waiting for her sullen daughter to catch up with her and her husband. The girl, aged about ten, was walking ever-so-slowly, making a laborious show of moving one foot in front of the other. At the rate she was going, it would take her an hour to catch up with her mum.

"Move!" said mum, angrier now. "Walk properly."

I passed the girl and mum. When I turned around a few metres ahead, I saw that mum was dragging the girl by her arm. San Marino, plainly, did not appeal to everyone.

I continued along the cliff top path known as the Witches' Pass. It was called this, because once upon a time, suspected witches had been dragged along the trail to a point where they could be flung from the cliffs. I looked around to see if I could spot the cackling woman from earlier but soon realised the futility in this. There were just too many people. I did notice the Japanese man though. We nodded at each other as we passed: fellow solo travellers.

I found an open-air bar and ordered a drink. With a view overlooking the landscape below (and the Adriatic in the far distance), I sipped on my 5.80 euro Titanbrau beer, shivered and pondered what to do next. I didn't have time for much because the bus back to Rimini was leaving in forty minutes, so I looked at the thin pamphlet about San Marino that someone had left on the table. Inside, I read something annoying: San Marino had two torture museums! One was a state-sanctioned museum full of ancient torturing equipment, featuring over 100 devices including the *skinning device*, the *heretics fork* and the simple but effective *knee-breaker*. The other torture museum was the one I'd visited.

I looked at my watch, and wondered whether I'd have time to visit the decent torture museum. Probably not. Instead, I finished my drink and stopped briefly at the marble-clad Basilica di San Marino, which supposedly contained the relics of Marinus, the city-state's founder. Then I loitered for a few minutes in a busy square dominated by the Palazzo Pubblico, the almost castle-like town hall. I took a photo of the huge Christmas tree opposite it and then made my way downhill toward the bus stops. The Japanese man was already there, as were the Chinese girls. Soon after, we were all sitting aboard the bus as it made its return journey to Rimini. After one more night in Bologna, I would be heading to the airport for my next port of call, where, if all went well, I'd be meeting up with Angela in Vienna.

Top row: One of the towers of San Marino City; The town hall tower
Middle row: Inside the lesser torture museum; A man regards the guns of San Marino
Bottom row: A church spire looks out over the distant hills of Italy; San Marino has a great collection of statues

Chapter 20. Vienna, Austria

Interesting fact: The oldest zoo in the world is in Vienna.

"This bloody blizzard!" I said to Angela as we traversed yet another slippery footpath, this one leading towards a bridge spanning the Danube. Snow was blasting into my eyes and the wind was chilling me to the bone. Angela was suffering too, but, like arctic explorers, we traipsed onto the bridge, pausing only to pull down our hats. I began to think I needed goggles and perhaps a pickaxe. The river below was dark and brooding, the cruise ships of the summer nowhere to be seen. Vienna in December was like being in Siberia.

2

Despite the weather, our first impressions of the Austrian capital were favourable. Beautiful, elegant buildings were on every street corner, no doubt from a time when the Hapsburgs ruled the land. Every now and again we would hear tinny police sirens (the type only heard in mainland Europe) and see red trams trundling along the city's streets. But then a blizzard would whitewash everything around us.

"Why did I let you convince me to join you here?" shouted Angela. I could barely hear her because my hat was covering my frostbitten ears. "Remind me again."

"Because it's Christmassy."

"No it's not. Christmassy is soft snow on the ground, it's children playing with sledges, it's Christmas market stalls selling mulled wine. Not...*this!*"

I had to agree that things were getting worse. Our coats were almost coated in white and our shoes had left large footprints behind us.

The sudden arctic blast over central Europe had caused a whitewash across the whole region, not just in Vienna. In fact, it had been touch and go whether we'd make it in from Italy. Angela's flight from Manchester had been delayed and so had mine, but in the end, things had worked out quite nicely; we had arrived into Austria at about the same time.

"My feet are freezing," announced Angela. "And so is my nose."

I tightened my scarf, trying to cover exposed areas of skin. My feet were freezing too. I looked around at the parked cars covered in snow, icicles hanging from their bumpers. And then I spied a cosy bakery through the tundra-like conditions. It looked warm and inviting, a respite from the cold with its tempting cakes and pastries. Like invaders from the north, we headed towards it.

3

Vienna, like most major European cities, has endured its fair share of foreign invaders. The Romans conquered it in 15 BC, and then the Turks laid siege in the sixteenth century. Napoleon came knocking on the city walls in 1805, and then, just before the outbreak of the Second World War, the Germans arrived and stayed put until the Red Army pushed them out in 1945.

Vienna was also no slouch when it came to famous people: Marie Antoinette, the Queen of France, was born in Vienna, and Sigmund Freud, the famous psychiatrist, carried out most of his important work in the city; Gustav Klimt, the symbolist painter was born near Vienna, and of course, there are the composers Franz Schubert and Johann Strauss, both sons of the city. Even Mozart, though not actually born in Vienna, settled in the city, living much of his life there.

Angela and I shook ourselves free of snow before we entered the cafe; we then stepped into the toasty interior, instantly taking in the aroma of freshly ground coffee. Christmas decorations were everywhere as we shuffled past a few other patrons, all seated and in deep pleasant conversation. After ordering some coffees, we sat by the window so we could keep abreast of the latest weather conditions. The snow was still falling heavily and we wondered whether it would ever actually stop.

"This is nice," I said, staring out and feeling my toes tingling due to the heat. Angela didn't say anything. I picked up my coffee and took a sip. It was exactly what the doctor ordered. Angela picked up her cup too.

"It's nice, isn't it?" I said again. "The coffee, I mean."

Angela looked at me and nodded. "You do realise," she said, "that your punishment for this will be the opera."

I raised my eyebrows. "The opera? What are you talking about?"

"Vienna is famous for the opera and I want to go tonight. Neither of us has been before and so your punishment for bringing me to Vienna during the worst snow blizzard in living memory is the opera. Okay?"

"But you'll be punishing yourself." I looked my wife squarely in the eyes, "Because, as far as I know, you're not an opera fan either."

"Well I am now. So that's settled."

I looked outside. The storm seemed to be easing. I could actually see across the street now. With everything coated in white, Vienna looked pretty. Even the dagger-like icicles hanging above the window were sparkling and glistening in a most pleasing way. I picked up the guidebook and began to flick through, reading about the opera.

4

Saint Stephen's Cathedral was a massive gothic-spired building that dated from the Middle Ages. Outside stood a man with a cart and two white horses. Not many customers for him, I reasoned; in fact, there seemed to be a huge lack of tourists, full stop. Maybe people had more sense than to come to Vienna in winter.

"Look at this," said Angela. We were inside the cathedral, in front of a particularly fetching sculpture showing a set of heads. "They look so lifelike." We both studied the intricate work of whoever the master craftsman had been. He'd carved the faces with utmost skill, except for one thing – the eyes. Where expression should have been was only a lifeless stare: the gaze of ghosts.

Nearby was a group of teenage girls following their guide. As they crowded around a sculpture a bit further along, one of the girls, I noticed, looked intensely bored by the whole thing. She stood a few metres back from her pals, looking sullen and resentful. I wasn't surprised when she produced a phone and checked it for messages. When the guide looked at her, she hid it but couldn't hide her yawn. She looked the typical teenager forced to do something boring; exactly how I'd have looked twenty years before.

Back outside, we trudged past well kept buildings that could easily have graced any period drama from the Napoleonic Age. And all of them looked fairy-tale pretty due to the fresh coatings of snow on their pointed rooftops. Men with spades were clearing the pavements while women wearing furry Russian-style hats and high heels click-clacked around them, dancing across the frosty cobbles and pavements.

Around the corner was the Vienna Opera House. Like most opera houses, it was large and grand, with the bonus of two horse statues on the roof. Resigned to buying tickets for the evening performance, I was delighted when the doors would not open. After staring at them for a moment, Angela tried them, but they wouldn't budge. And that was when I noticed the sign saying the opera house was closed for the week.

"Bloody hell," I said. "I was looking forward to it as well. I can't believe it's closed."

"Don't," snapped Angela.

"Don't what?"

"You know exactly what I mean. So just don't."

I decided to keep mute. I also tried not to smile. It wasn't easy.

5

We arrived at the Hofburg Imperial Palace. Sitting on the top, like bulbous green helmets, were three gigantic domes. It was a scene of pure dynastic opulence. As if on cue, a horse and carriage clip-clopped under one of the large archways.

Once the home of Habsburg Kings, the imperial palace is now the official residence of the Austrian President, Heinz Fischer. We followed a line of small school children being carefully shepherded under the arch by their teacher. Their destination was the nearby Spanish Riding School, where the world famous Lipizzaner Horses performed. We passed through into a beautiful courtyard where we stopped to look at the map.

"We can either go to the old hospital museum or we can go for a Sachertorte."

Angela thought for a moment. "Sachertorte."

"I thought you'd say that."

After a shortcut through a park, where we managed to stumble across a golden statue of Johan Strauss, we arrived at Cafe Sacher Wien. Its interior was posh, full of crystal chandeliers, olden-days' paintings and tiny tables. It looked like the sort of place where posh people could enjoy a slice of posh cake.

In 1832, a young man called Franz Sacher had devised Sachertorte, the famous chocolate cake that came with a hint of apricot sauce. At the age of sixteen, Sacher had been thrust into the cake-making limelight when his boss, the chief cook of the Austrian Minister of Foreign Affairs, was taken down with an ailment so debilitating that he had to go home and leave his apprentice in charge. On a normal day, this would have been bad enough, but, on the day of his illness, the minister's household was expecting important guests, and so the fear factor was notched up to ten. In addition, the kitchen had been told to create a dessert so special that it would be the talk of the town. And so upon Sacher's young shoulders this order now rested.

With bated breath, waiters served the guests the cake. In the kitchens, it is reasonable to assume that Franz Sacher would have been shaking like a leaf. But he needn't have worried; his dessert went down a storm, and proved so popular that Sacher became famous. When he died in 1907, his son took over the lucrative Sachertorte-making business and went on to establish the cafe in which Angela and I were now sitting.

Two plates arrived and were set down on the table in front of us. The thick slice of chocolate cake with a generous dollop of whipped cream looked tasty enough, but, then again, for five pounds each, I would have expected nothing less. I wasted no time in cutting into my slice and stuffed a large piece in my mouth. It went down the hatch without touching the sides. It was delicious: the slight touch of apricot really added to the whole flavoursome experience. But was it that special? I didn't think so and neither did Angela. And when the waiter demanded a euro each to retrieve our coats from the hanger, the taste soured further. Still, we were glad we'd tried the cake; sampling Sachertorte in Vienna is as essential as trying a Danish pastry in Copenhagen.

6

Narrenturn turned out to be a large round tower located in the University district. We joined the short queue and came face to face with the monstrosities on display inside the former asylum. Distorted skeletons (one clearly of a small child with a massively oversized skull), diseased lungs and plastic mock-ups of people with all sorts of deformities were all on show. Thank God the captions were in German.

The circular museum had once been next to Vienna General Hospital; whenever doctors suspected someone was mentally deficient, they would send them next door. Because of the type of patients it used to house, it became known as the Fool's Tower, and, in its heyday, in the late eighteenth century, it contained 139 cells, each with sturdy barred doors to block escape. Most of the rooms were now full of exhibits.

"Jesus Christ," I said, as we entered one of the gruesome rooms. In front of us were plastic models of hideously diseased genitalia. One penis had a shaft full of angry sores, a vagina had red welts and some indescribable protrusions, and, in one graphic picture, a penis had something unspeakable oozing from its tip.

Another room was worse. It contained three actual babies contained in formaldehyde jars. One infant looked like it had been born the day before: its poor eyes were squeezed shut and its tiny mouth was open slightly, as if taking its first breath. Why it was in the jar we had no idea – because as far as we could tell, the infant looked normal and healthy – and because of this, it soon became hard to look at. The other two jars were equally horrible, both containing hellishly deformed babies. One looked to have been triplets, all merged into one body. I felt nauseous looking and left the room, wandering around the other exhibits in a sort of daze.

"Well, that was fun," said Angela as we left the museum thirty minutes later. Even though the exhibits had been at best macabre, and, at worst, disturbing, it had been well worth the three euro entrance fee, even if we did feel like vomiting. We headed back into the town centre.

7

I felt like vomiting later that evening too, though for a very different reason. Just near our hotel (we didn't want to venture too far because the snow had started again) was a nice-looking restaurant where we both ordered enchiladas.

"Bloody hellfire!" I exclaimed as I took a forkful of my meal. The enveloping taste of prime garlic filled every pore of my mouth, immediately rendering my breath venomous to everyone in the vicinity. Everything on the plate was coated with the stuff, even the peas, and, as I dipped my fork in for another try of Garlic Hell, my nausea returned. "My stomach will end up as an exhibit in that museum," I said, immediately covering my mouth to halt the escape of foul gas inside my innards.

Angela too commented on the amount of garlic used in the recipe. I remained mute as I chewed a piece of chicken that had been stewed in garlic for at least forty-eight years. I looked down at my plate, mentally calculating how many cloves of garlic per square inch had been deposited on my plate. There was a coating of white cream everywhere, clearly the source of the hideous sauce. Even the beer couldn't wash away the foul taste.

"So what do you want to do tomorrow?" Angela asked. "Before our flight to Frankfurt, I mean."

I shrugged, poking about on my plate. I was trying to remove the excess sauce as best I could. "I'm not sure."

"Well, how about we go to the Belvedere Palace? Part of it is showing a Klimt exhibition. I'd like to see that, seeing as we didn't get to see an opera."

I tentatively took another mouthful of my enchilada. Within a nanosecond, the cloves of garlic worked their black magic and filled my taste buds with something only an Italian grandmother should ever taste. I put my fork down and pushed the plate away. "Fine. Klimt it is."

8

Our final day in Vienna began with another cold and snowy morning. I could still detect a strong sense of garlic on my breath; undaunted, we wrapped up warm and undertook a lengthy walk through the snow towards Schloss Belvedere, an eighteenth century palace built for Prince Eugene of Savoy, who was apparently Austria's most successful general. Another interesting fact was that Franz Ferdinand had lived there until his untimely assassination in 1914.

Large and white, with a splendid green roof, Schloss Belvedere looked every inch the palace it was; being located in an area all by itself made its grandeur seem even more magnificent. Even the large hedges at its front added to the appeal. They had been shaped into spheres; with their white tops of snow, they looked like frosted cupcakes.

After shaking our feet, we entered the section of the palace set aside as a museum. Art by the likes of Munch, Van Gogh, and, best of all, Gustav Klimt was there to see.

"I really want to see *The Kiss*," Angela told me. "It's one of Klimt's best."

"How come you suddenly know so much about art?"

"I don't. But I do know about Klimt. I studied his work at college."

Paintings of cherubs, scenes of nude women lounging about, large pictures of turkeys and even intricately detailed portraits of farmers' wives were just some of the subjects on offer. In one strange room, sculptures of men's heads in various poses stood on plinths. The sculptor was a man called Franz Xaver Messerschmitt, best known for the *Character Heads* at which we were now gaping. The caption underneath one read: 'Saved from drowning, face'. Another read: 'Injured in Battle, face. The description of the faces summed up the expressions perfectly.

On the second floor was the exhibition we had come to see – the world's largest collection of Klimt paintings. His masterwork, *The Kiss,* was on prominent display, all glittering with gold leaf. A group of people were standing around it with a studious-looking male guide. Edging closer, we listened in as he began to speak.

"This is the pinnacle of Klimt's career," the guide said in English, "and it is believed to show Klimt and his lover in an embrace, which is significant for two reasons. The first is that the lady in question was about to leave Klimt – he had been adulterous and had caught syphilis. Understandably, this didn't make her too happy." The guide paused, pointing to the bottom section of the painting. "You may notice that the woman's legs are quite long here, and that, if she were to stand up, she would be taller than Klimt..."

We all looked. Now that the guide had pointed them out, the legs did appear to be unnaturally long. I would never have noticed it if the guide had not made the observation.

The guide continued. "Klimt did this for a special reason: he wanted to show that she was a *better* person than him; she held the moral high ground."

I glanced at my watch. We had to make tracks. We had an afternoon flight to catch to Frankfurt. We left the guide and his group of art lovers and went back outside, slipping and sliding in the snow once more. Austria had been ticked off the list, and now it was time for Germany.

Top row: Schloss Belvedere; Delicious Sachertorte
Middle row: One of the monstrosities inside the Narrenturn
Museum; Johan Strauss and Me; Saint Stephen's Cathedral
Bottom row: Inside a courtyard of the Hofburg Imperial
Palace; Angela posing outside the town hall

Chapter 21: Frankfurt, Germany

Interesting fact: Hot Dogs, a Frankfurt invention, are responsible for 17% of food-related asphyxiations in American children under the age of ten.

"Why aren't the trains as good as this in England?" said Angela as we sped towards the centre of Frankfurt. Outside was rainy and overcast but inside was warm and snug. I shook my head, wondering the same thing. Everywhere else in the world, it seemed, from Belarus to Peru, had a better railway system than the UK. It was embarrassing, especially since the airport train we were travelling in was spotlessly clean, exactly on time, and more importantly, cheap as chips.

Half an hour later, after dropping our bags in our room, we headed along a street lined with bakeries and clothes shops. The former were pouring delicious smells into the street, selling the last of their wares before they closed for the day; the latter were already closed. We came to a fetching building, which turned out to be another opera house. Instead of trying to get tickets, we simply took refuge under its awnings to escape the wind and rain.

"Those skyscrapers look impressive," I said as I thrust my hands into my pockets. The almost ethereal silver towers had their top sections covered in cloud. Frankfurt was one of the power houses of the German economy where all the major banks had their headquarters.

When the rain subsided sufficiently for us to move on, we stopped at another tower, this one much older than the skyscrapers of Frankfurt's financial district. The Eschenheim Tower dated from medieval times and was once part of the old town's fortifications. With its tall round tower and spiky turrets, it looked exactly the sort of place a dastardly baron would have imprisoned a beautiful princess. In the early nineteenth century, the tower had been earmarked for demolition along with all the other old walls and towers. It was only spared because a French ambassador at the time stepped in and asked for it to remain in place.

"Have you noticed the holes in the weather vane?" I asked, pointing at the top of the tower.

Angela looked at the yellow flag-like vane, which contained a circular pattern of holes. "What about them?"

"In the Middle Ages there was a poacher who was put in prison inside the tower. Poaching was a serious crime in those days, and the poor bloke was facing the noose."

"The noose? Just for poaching?"

"Yeah, and according to legend, on the ninth day of his incarceration, the poacher offered the courts a strange bet: if he could shoot nine holes in the flag, one for each day he'd been in prison, they should set him free; if he missed, even just one, he would willingly go to the gallows. They agreed and watched as he took aim. He got every one and they had to set him free. And that's why the weather vane has holes in it."

"I dare you to kiss Santa," jibed Angela. Father Christmas was standing outside a pharmacy just around the corner and seemed to be by himself. I quickly scoped out the area and decided it was safe enough to take on the dare. Nonchalantly, I walked over to Santa while Angela waited nearby, camera at the ready, a wry smile on her face. After checking that the coast was clear and making sure that no one was watching from inside the pharmacy, I rushed up to Santa and placed a smacker on his bristly, but clearly plastic, face. That done, we returned to the hotel for the evening.

2

The next morning, we walked to the old town, to the start of the Christmas market where the yuletide factor was upped big style. There was enough festiveness to quicken the heart of even the grimmest of Christmas haters. Angela was almost giddy with excitement.

The rich aroma of mulled wine and sweet cinnamon filled the air as we walked around the stalls. Long strips of candy dangled from some, and, at others, sparkly stars spun in the breeze. Further in, a colourful carousel filled with giggling children spun to the sound of Christmas music; everywhere we cared to look, beeswax candles, wooden toys and glistening trinkets were for sale in stalls decorated with frosted snowflakes and wooden Christmas trees.

"Even you," said Angela, "must agree that this looks good."

I was someone who could quite happily give Christmas a miss. Not quite a detester of the festive period, I was nonetheless a person who couldn't find much joy in putting up a Christmas tree and found the prospect of wrapping gifts a right royal pain in the neck. The thought of battling the masses to buy presents could bring me out in a sweat, and then there was the niggling problem of what to buy anyway. Besides, the joy of Christmas had left me aged twelve when my dog died on Christmas Day. The tree fell on top of her, short-circuiting some lights; you can guess the rest.

I made that last bit up: we didn't even have a dog. But you get the picture. However, Angela was quite correct about the scene before us – it did look fetching and ever so Christmassy. Underneath a parade of twinkling Christmas lights and sparkly snowflakes, a girl aged about eight looked about as excited as anyone I'd ever seen. Who could blame her? If ever there was a scene to epitomise Christmas, then this was it; the only thing missing was the snow. Vienna had taken it.

3

"I want sausage!" I announced as we browsed the aisles. "Prime, juicy, German sausage!"

Sausages featured heavily inside the market. They were available to buy either as cold wrapped tubes, or else hot, cooked upon large griddles by men with thick moustaches. The latter were selling particularly well and the tempting smells were floating all around us.

"Why don't we have some mulled wine first?" suggested Angela.

The warming liquid came in a colourful little cup that warmed our cockles, whatever they were. We found a quiet corner and sipped the spiced wine, watching a large carousel revolving to the tunes of Christmas songs.

"How long have we got before we have to head to the airport?" Angela asked. I was busy watching a strange looking couple. Both were in their late fifties and wearing identical backpacks. The woman was short and round, the man tall and thin like a beanpole. He was a good foot taller than his wife, and also had a long scraggly beard and a monk's bowl-type haircut. They certainly made an odd couple, but, like us, they were enjoying their own mulled wines.

"An hour and a half," I said. I took another sip of the warm wine. I could feel it heating my insides as it made its way down my gullet. If a cold beer was the perfect drink for a hot afternoon, then mulled wine was the perfect drink on a wintry morning. "So we had better get moving if we want to see much more."

We finished our drinks and set off walking.

4

In the main square, Romerberg, the Christmas market continued unabated, all under the watchful eye of a giant Christmas tree. Triangular roofs and wooden beams crisscrossed rows of tiny windows; it all looked suitably medieval, even though the buildings dated from the 1980s. The Allies had flattened the originals during the Second World War.

Just south of the square was the River Main, a wide strip of grey spanned by a few bridges. We crossed one and stopped in the middle, looking down at the few boats tethered for the winter. I heard some squawking and a general hubbub from below. A woman was surrounded by a flock of swirling gulls, together with a platoon of swans who had emerged from the river flapping their wings in consternation. As we watched, she flung a few bits of bread from a plastic bag and the birds went mental. It was like a scene from a Hitchcock movie. We could hardly see the woman due to the tight jumble of beaks, wings and feathers. A swan entered the fray and came out with a snapping beak full of bread.

Angela nudged me. She was pointing to some padlocks attached to the railings of the bridge. Each one was engraved with names and a date, placed there on a couple's wedding day, we presumed. Now that we'd noticed them, we saw that virtually the whole bridge was covered in padlocks of every shape and size. One read: Salim & Yvonne, 28.10.09.

"I wonder if they're still married," I asked.

"Yeah. That would be interesting to know." I sniffed the air again. I could smell sausage.

5

We joined the queue at the large circular stall that seemed the most popular. A man in a white apron was turning long tubes of meat over on the griddle. The smell was delicious, and soon enough Angela had purchased one large sausage inside a small roll of bread. After pressing on a dollop of tomato ketchup from the dispenser, I took a large bite. It was as scrumptious as promised and I passed it to Angela so she could try some.

Angela took a healthy bite. "Mmm. Very nice. German sausage is wunderbar!"

When we finished, we found our need for sausage was not sated. This time we wanted some cold ones to take back home with us. We headed through the Christmas market until we found a stall that sold hundreds of them. Similar to the store I'd come across back in Luxembourg, sausages were everywhere: dangling from the rafters above our eye line, laid out in neat rows below us, or stacked up like tiny missiles behind the proprietor. When we stopped to regard the man's wares, he asked where we were from.

"England," I said.

The man nodded solemnly. "Not the best place for sausage," he said, his accent heavy and deep. "English sausages are all limp and pink, yah? Not like the German sausage. Thick and firm! Tell me, which do you prefer?" He glanced at Angela.

Angela pointed at a sausage dangling at the front of his stall. "What are those ones like?"

The man grinned. "All my sausage iz good, Yah! Prime meat and goodness. And the sausage you are pointing at is one of my best. If you like, I can slice some off the end so you can taste it yourself."

Angela shook her head. "No, we'll take your word for it. We'll have ten, please"

The man raised his hairy eyebrows. "Ten? Are you sure? Perhaps you want to try more from my stock."

"No," Angela said. "Those ones are fine. They'll be gifts for people back home."

I was thinking about how we would get them through customs intact. Hadn't the EU banned meat products from crossing borders? But it was too late to ponder such things because Angela was handing over a twenty-euro note.

The man wrapped the sausages up in white paper and passed them over with our change. He grinned at me. "For you, I have included one extra sausage. I hope you like."

We thanked him and walked away with our bounty. When we'd gone a sufficient distance, I turned to Angela. "Was he for real? I mean, he sounded like a character from an *Allo, Allo* sketch! Meaty sausages, and a special one just for me. What was that about?"

Angela laughed.

We headed for the train station so we could return to the airport. We would be spending Christmas in the UK with our family for a week before flying off to the final stop on the rapid-fire trek of Western Europe. New Year's Eve would be celebrated Finnish style: a fitting end to our West European adventure, we both hoped.

Top row: Decorations in the Christmas Market; A mixture of old and new – the Eschenheim Tower and modern skyscrapers
Middle row: Mulled wine; Frankfurt's old town is gorgeous
Bottom row: German sausage; Down by the river

Chapter 22. Helsinki, Finland

Interesting fact: There are no public payphones in Finland.

Angela and I sat in the departure lounge of Manchester Airport. I felt like I'd been spending half my life in airports recently, and the experience had long since descended into one of queues, security searches, grabbing expensive coffees and looking at departure boards for gate numbers. Airports and air travel were a necessary evil.

"So this is the final stop on our travels around Western Europe. Thank God," I said.

"People think it's glamorous," Angela replied. "It's anything but."

"I think air travel stopped being glamorous in the 1980s. But at least we are flying Finnair, a *real* airline, this time. Remember that one we flew on to Lisbon?"

"Don't remind me."

I looked at the people around us. Despite it being eight thirty in the morning, the number of people supping on pints of beer was insane. I wondered whether it was a British institution – having a pint as soon as you arrived at the airport – or whether tattooed people everywhere did it; I doubted it.

"Do you realise," I said, "that when we approach Finland, we'll begin a descent into Hell...sinki!"

Angela rolled her eyes. "Rubbish."

I picked up my pint of lager and took a large gulp. Except it was a latte, of course. The thought of a pint at this time of the morning made my stomach lurch. I glanced at the board again. Twenty minutes until boarding.

2

The airport bus to central Helsinki was painless and cheap. Even better was the location of our hotel, right in the centre of the city. It was already dark by the time we arrived; after checking in, we decided to eat in the hotel restaurant. Afterwards, we retired to our room to watch a DVD. We wanted to be rested for the big day ahead.

The next morning, New Year's Eve, we got up, had breakfast and ventured outside. The sky was gloomy and overcast – the sort of day we knew would never really improve, and, though it was already ten in the morning, the high latitude of Finland meant the sun had been up for less than an hour.

"I couldn't live here," Angela said, as we walked towards the centre. "I need more sunlight than this. When is sunset?"

"About twenty past three."

My wife did a mental calculation. "So only six and a half hours of daylight? No!"

Though there wasn't any snow and frost underfoot, it was still bloody cold; it was spitting with bitter rain too. Everyone was wrapped up like Eskimos, but most looked in good cheer, perhaps buoyed by the thought of the evening's festivities.

As expected, Finland's capital looked well kept, with grand buildings and fancy Christmas lights all over the place. "Watch out," said Angela, pulling me back onto the pavement. A city tram rushed past, a blur of green and white, its passengers' faces gone in a second.

"Jesus!"

"I don't know how you haven't been knocked over. You never watch where you're going. Remember that one in Lisbon?"

We reached Senate Square, with the imposing green-domed Helsinki Cathedral standing at one end. Built in 1852, this magnificent cathedral was a major tourist draw in the summer months, but in the depths of winter, there were hardly any tourists at all. In the square below it, gangs of men were busy setting up stages and a large screen in time for the night's celebration. That evening, we'd return with the crowds, but for now, we wrapped our scarves tighter, pulled down our hats and headed for pastures new.

3

"I never liked the Moomins," I said as we stopped at a statue of one outside a shop. Someone, presumably the shop owners, had placed a hat on the creature. The Moomins were big and white creatures that looked like friendly hippos. Created by Finnish author Tove Jansson in the 1940s, the Moomins cartoons are one of Finland's most famous exports.

"Me neither. But I think we were either too old or too young to appreciate them." Angela looked at the sky. The spitting had turned to drizzle. With the low cloud base and the lack of light, it seemed like it was late evening.

We left the Moomin and headed towards the presidential palace, along the way passing the enormous Uspenski Cathedral, the largest Orthodox Cathedral in Western Europe. "Have you noticed the people?" I said, as we strolled down a busy street towards the harbour front.

"What about them?"

"Their physical features, I mean. Most have dark hair, not blonde, like in Sweden or Denmark. They look like that singer from Iceland...what's her name...Bjork."

Angela had another look. "I see what you mean." A trio of young women were walking past, all black hair and angular features.

A couple of grey-uniformed guards were standing to attention outside the enormous white presidential palace, which in its time had been a military hospital, a home of Russian Czars (Finland had been a Grand Duchy of the Russian Empire) and briefly a Finnish royal residence. The guards seemed oblivious to the cold temperatures.

"How old are they?" I quipped. "Fifteen?"

Angela smiled. "That's a sure sign of getting old: thinking that soldiers and policemen look too young."

I nodded. To escape the worst of the rain, we crossed the road to Market Square, browsing the fish, honey, cheese and touristy souvenirs for sale. We were the only people there apart from an old couple who were checking out the fish; after shivering around a few stalls, and not seeing anything worth buying, we went to get some lunch.

4

For what remained of the afternoon, we decided to visit the small island of Suomenlinna. The ferry terminal was at the other end of Market Square; when we got there, an electronic display informed us that the ferry was leaving in less than one minute.

Suomenlinna Island is a sea fortress dating from the eighteenth century. Prior to the Russians taking over, Finland had been under Swedish control, and it was they who had built the barracks, fortifications and tunnels on the island in an attempt to block any oncoming Russian warships. It was all a waste of time, though: the Russians took the island after only the briefest bombardment.

Fifteen minutes after setting off, the ferry arrived onto the bleak and rocky island. As well as the fortress walls, old cannons and windswept beaches, Suomenlinna contained a few homes, a handful of shops, a prison and a large church that stood in the middle of the island. What made the church interesting was its dome. It looked standard issue except for one important detail: at night, it continuously flashed a Morse code signal for the letter 'H' for Helsinki. According to the information placard, Suomenlinna Church doubled as a lighthouse – apparently the only one in the world.

Nowadays, 900 permanent residents (including a set of low-security prisoners) inhabit Suomenlinna Island, with most of the prisoners being responsible for the general upkeep of the old fortifications. Whether any of the cons were working that day, we couldn't tell, but if they were, I felt sorry for them – the island was getting a good battering from the elements. Freezing rain was blowing in from the Baltic, and so when Angela and I reached the southern end of the island and saw nothing but a cauldron of grey, we decided enough was enough. We headed back to the ferry terminal.

5

One thing we noticed about Helsinki was that it was noticeably cheaper than the other Scandinavian capitals (with the exception of Reykjavik). A cup of coffee was not a splurge item to break the bank and a beer, though expensive, was just about bearable. Even so, we were glad we'd bought a small bottle of gin in duty free, and, after purchasing some tonic water from a supermarket, we returned to the hotel to mix it together. That done, we put it in the fridge to chill.

"Are you going to try your banana?" asked Angela.

I nodded, picking it up, turning the strange fruit over in my hands. I'd not seen a red banana before, so, when I had spotted one in the supermarket, I simply had to buy it. It was smaller and thicker than a normal banana. I tentatively peeled back its skin, wondering what it would look like inside and was slightly disappointed when it looked normal and yellow.

Its taste was different, though; whether my red banana was from a bad bunch, or simply under-ripe, the resulting sudden drying of my mouth left me literally open-mouthed. One small bite of a red banana had left me parched beyond belief.

"What's it like?" asked Angela."

I chewed and swallowed the saliva-destroying piece of banana. The taste was bitter too. "Horrible. It's sucked all moisture from my mouth. I'm chucking the rest of it away."

By 10.30 pm, we were ready to hit the town. Wrapped up warm, armed with our bottle of pre-made gin and tonic, we stepped outside. On the dark streets of Helsinki, we could hear the bangs and whistles of fireworks going off in the distance. It was time to meet the New Year head on.

6

We arrived back at Senate Square as the crowds began arriving. The cathedral was illuminated like a beacon, and to its left, on the main stage, there were five male singers dressed in suits, crooning something in Finnish. With over an hour to go before midnight, and not wanting to hang around in the minus-three conditions, we decided to find a bar to keep warm. We found a nice one overlooking the harbour.

"I like Helsinki better than Copenhagen," said Angela, taking a sip of her wine. "But it's not as nice as Stockholm."

The bar was full of festive revellers. But unlike in the UK, everyone was well behaved, despite the relatively late hour. Plus, there was a healthy mix of young and old. It looked like a good crowd.

"Where are you from?" said a man sitting at the next table along. He had a walrus moustache and a large pint of lager in his hand. His wife was sitting next to him, smiling at us. She had a pint too, but instead of a moustache, she favoured red lipstick.

"England," I answered. "Where are you from?"

"Finland!"

I nodded in appreciation, wondering what to say next. The woman was still grinning and both seemed slightly inebriated. I looked at Angela, who picked up her glass of wine. Finally, I said, "It's a lovely country."

They both seemed to consider this and then nodded thoughtfully. The man took a slurp of his lager. It was almost gone. "But very cold in winter, yes?"

Angela decided to step into the conversation. "Yes, but not as cold as Vienna was last week."

"Vienna?" asked the man. "You are from Vienna?"

"No," answered Angela, "we're from England. But we were in Vienna just before Christmas."

The man looked at his wife and then back to us. "Well nice meeting you, but we must go. We have a party to attend."

As they got up to leave, I looked at Angela and raised my eyebrows. "Another confusing conversation with someone from a different country to add to the collection."

7

With only minutes to go before the New Year, we jostled for position among the crowds in Senate Square. It was an eager crowd, especially with a man on the stage whipping up every bit of excitement as the hour crept closer. People were smiling and laughing, posing for photos and looking expectantly at the large digital display that was counting down the minutes and seconds.

I took a large swig of gin and tonic and passed the bottle to Angela. She did the same, no doubt feeling the heat as the liquid made its way downwards. And then the man with the microphone suddenly started chanting what we presumed to be the ten-second countdown. A building crescendo of cheering, whistling and clapping began to fill the whole square. The locals around us joined in with the oral countdown, some jumping up and down in time to each stroke of the clock. Then midnight chimed. There was an almighty roar from the crowd and the fireworks began.

"Happy New Year!" I roared in Angela's direction, trying to make myself heard over the cascading rockets above our heads.

"Happy New Year to you!" Angela shouted back. All around, people were hugging, kissing, and spinning around, taking in the fireworks blasting and exploding in the sky. And then as quickly as they had started, the celebrations died down. The fireworks stopped (though we could still hear the odd stray firecracker going off in the streets around us) and some tinny pop music began blaring out over the square. Ten minutes later, as people began to move away, we followed, making our way through the night-time streets of downtown Helsinki. Half an hour later, we arrived back at the hotel, and after a quick nightcap in the bar, we retired for the night, pleased we had seen in the New Year, Scandinavian-style. It had been a fitting way to end our travels through Western Europe.

8

"Out of all the places you went to – with me and by yourself – which is your favourite?" asked Angela.

We were sitting in the departure lounge of Helsinki-Vantaa International Airport. Over the past six months, airports and departure lounges had merged into one. I'd lost count of the number of flights, buses and trains I'd travelled in as I'd hopped in and around Western Europe. I thought about it for a moment. There were so many to choose from: twenty-two to be exact. And each one had shown me something new, from nude statues in Oslo to beautiful riverside settings in Zurich, from the crowds of Rome and the Vatican to the smallness of Liechtenstein and San Marino.

I finally spoke. "Western Europe has offered a lot, but my favourite, I think, would either be Monaco or Reykjavik."

Angela replied, "Mine is Lisbon. I could live in Lisbon."

We both fell silent, thinking our own thoughts about our travels. We had conquered Western Europe. And our bank balance had survived the onslaught. But only just.

*Top left: Me standing in Senate Square; The Presidential
Palace
Middle row: Looking out from the battlements on Suomenlinna
Island; The Lighthouse Church on Suomenlinna Island; A couple
of Moomin mugs
Bottom row: Uspenski Cathedral and harbour*

If you have enjoyed this book by Jason Smart, perhaps you will also like his other books, which are all available from Amazon.

The Red Quest
Flashpacking through Africa
The Balkan Odyssey
Temples, Tuk-tuks and Fried Fish Lips
Panama City to Rio de Janeiro
Bite Size Travel in North America
Crowds, Colour, Chaos
Rapid Fire Europe
Meeting the Middle East
From Here to Anywhere
Take Your Wings and Fly

Visit his website www.theredquest.com for more details.

19640361R00148

Printed in Poland
by Amazon Fulfillment
Poland Sp. z o.o., Wrocław